I Will Die Tomorrow, But Not Today

Memoirs of

BERNARD (BERL) SCHUSTER

Winterman Ink

The articles on pages 71 and 79 were originally published in *The Daily Record*
in Rochester, NY on December 26, 1996 and July 24, 2000 respectively.
They are reprinted with permission.

The article on page 72 originally appeared in the *Democrat and Chronicle*
in Rochester, NY on May 2, 1997. It is reprinted with permission.

The article on page 75 was originally published in the *Jewish Ledger*
in Rochester, NY on April 15, 1993. It is reprinted with permission.

International Standard Book Number (ISBN)
paper: 1-884299-07-5
cloth: 1-884399-04-0

Published by:
Winterman Ink
1595 Elmwood Avenue
Rochester, NY 14620-3602

Designer: Karen Burns/Birdsey Graphic Design, Waterloo, NY

For my Grandchildren
Christie, Sarah, Rachel, Saul and Laura

Christie

From left with Grandpa:
Sarah Elizabeth, Rachel Ann and Saul Benjamin

Laura

Dedicated to My Parents, Brother And Sisters

Who Did Not Survive The Holocaust

And Whose Love And Nurturing

Gave Me The Strength to Survive And Tell This Story.

Acknowledgments

I wish to thank the following individuals who assisted in the writing and publishing of this book:

First and foremost, my wife, Jane, proofread and edited this manuscript and, most of all, encouraged me during this project.

My mother-in-law, Rose Moress Presberg, accepted me into her family, and supported this project from beginning to end.

My son, Jamie, spent many hours digitizing pictures, laying out our family tree and giving me valuable advice.

My daughter, Deborah, often helped, encouraging me to continue on.

My dear friend, Charlie DeMarco, converted old photographs into color prints.

Margie Baker Price read my manuscripts and made many wonderful suggestions.

My friend, Randi L. Winterman, who gave so much of herself to this project that my gratitude is enormous and unending.

And, finally, my granddaughter, Sarah, whose begging "Grandpa, tell me about when you were a little boy..." started this project and has made everything worthwhile.

Chronology

May 17, 1928	Born in Jasionowka, Poland
1932	Moved to our house on Colonia Street
1939	The Germans and the Soviet Union divided Poland, and Jasionowka was occupied by Germany. One week later, the Soviet Union occupied the town.
1941	Germans attacked the Soviet Union and reoccupied Jasionowka
1941-1942	Created hiding place in porch and above the tannery
1/43	Tried to escape with father. Mother and youngest sister, Tzipe, were killed by the Germans.
2/43-8/44	Hid in the woods with Ruvak and Chone Goniondzky and a third man from our town.
11/44-12/44	Jasionowka liberated
1945	En Route to Palestine
11/26/46	Shot and admitted to Hospital in diLeuca
5/12/47	Sailed on Marine Perch from Naples, Italy to the US
5/22/47	Arrived in New York City
6/47	Traveled to Rochester, NY to live with my aunt, Mary Kaufman
1948	Received my high school diploma in just one year
1948-52	Attended University of Rochester
1952-55	Attended Harvard Law School
1955-57	Clerked for the New York State Court of Appeals
7/3/55	Married Jane Moress
4/14/58	Birth of our first child—Deborah Lee
1961	Formed law firm partnership with Francis Claus and Willard Curry
1/-1/61	Birth of son—James
3/8/64	Birth of daughter—Miriam Lynne
8/70	Frank A. Schwartzman joined the law firm of Claus, Curry and Schuster
7/75	Baile Schuster Gonionzki (sister) died in Australia
6/78	Feitche Schuster (sister) died in Guadalajara
4/94	Schleime Schuster (cousin and husband to Feitche) died in Israel
July 17, 2000	Berl died after a long battle with cancer at his home, surrounded by his loving family

Contents

Front row, from left to right: My sister Dverke, my mother Sarah, my father Jacob and my sister Baile.

Back row: My sisters Feitche and Mariashe and my brother Maier.

This picture was taken about 1920, some eight years before I was born.

PREFACE

A journey of 10,000 miles eventually must start with a first step, and taking that first step is often very difficult. Ever since you, Sarah, were 2 years old you have loved to hear stories, and not just stories found in fable books or stories that came from the imagination of talented people. Often you would say "Grandpa, tell me a story about when you were a little boy." I would put you to sleep by telling you stories about life in Jasionowka, the *shtetl* (town) in Poland where I was born. You never tired of hearing the names of my family members, and you were thrilled when you first learned that you were named after my mother, Sarah, may she rest in peace. I recall how happy you were to hear that your daddy, Jamie, (in Hebrew, Yakov or Jacob) was named after my father, Jacob (in Yiddish, Jankl), may he rest in peace. No sooner did you learn to speak, and you started to speak at a very early age, when you asked me to tell you the names of my sisters and brothers so that you could repeat each name very carefully:

Baile	Born 1908
Feitche	Born 11/5/1911
Mariashe	Born 1913
Maier	Born 1916
Dverke	Born 1920
Tzipe	Born 1922
Maishe	Born 5/5/1924

After I would say "Maishe," you, Sarah, always added, "and you, Grandpa Berl."

It is my hope that soon you, Saul Benjamin, will start to ask me to tell you the stories that your sister Sarah loves to hear. I don't know how many times I have told you, Sarah, the story about when Grandpa Berl got his new suit dirty and full of mud and received a spanking for doing so.

In hopes that you, children, will continue to love the stories from my past, and that someday when you are grown up and have children of your own, you will re-tell the stories to your children, I have resolved to put some of my recollections on paper and have included excerpts from my sister Feitche's journal.

My sister Feitche (Rosenbloom) Schuster, the second oldest of my siblings, survived the Holocaust with the help of a Polish family who gave her, her mother-in-law, our oldest sister Baile, and Baile's daughter, Roske, shelter. Feitche kept a diary which she rewrote in 1945 and produced a manuscript soon after we were liberated while the details were fresh in her mind. That manuscript, written in beautiful Yiddish, I have donated to the Holocaust Museum in Washington. I had it translated into English in 1982. I am attaching a copy because it describes in great detail what happened in Jasionowka during the period of German occupation. Feitche detailed the crimes and atrocities committed against us by our Polish neighbors and the Germans much better than I could ever hope to do. I was only a child during this period, whereas Feitche, some seventeen years older than I, knew everyone in town and had the wisdom and courage to record it all as it happened.

You, children, have been the joy of my life. There are many kinds of love and most are wonderful. The love I have felt and feel for all of you is indescribable. I firmly believe that the past difficulties I was subjected to as a child and youngster were worth it, so long as life included the joys and blessings that you have bestowed upon me, just by being my grandchildren. I feel very, very blessed.

As I write this, I am past 65 years of age, and the recollections I search for happened long, long ago and far away. I am no longer sure that what I think I recollect actually happened as I remember it. I think it is common knowledge that we repress some memories which are painful and "edit" recollections in order to help us cope. A short time ago a friend of mine, Ruvak Degani, with whom I grew up in Jasionowka and who shared my fate and destiny during the Holocaust, came to visit. Ruvak now lives in Israel. I was amazed to find how much his recollections of major events in my life during that period differed from my own recollections. The passage of time and perhaps our defense mechanisms seem to have worked on the memory of each of us. Just the same, I will make an effort to tell you, my dearest grandchildren, the story of my childhood as best I can.

Bernard Schuster

Rochester, NY

HUMBLE BEGINNINGS

I was born the eighth child to Sarah Maretzki and Jacob (Jankl) Schuster on May 17, 1928. I believe my parents did not plan my birth and were quite surprised when my mother, no longer young, became pregnant four years after her seventh child, Maishe, was born. By the time I arrived on the scene, my oldest sister, Baile, was just about ready to be married and have a family of her own. Thus, I became an uncle at the age of 3 when my niece Roske (now Rose Schwartz of Melbourne, Australia) was born.

Bernie — Age 4

When I was very little, my sister Baile, her husband, and Roske lived in the same house with us, and later in a house next to us, and I actually considered Roske as my sister. As a child, Roske was delicate and not very strong. To help her stay healthy and well nourished, her parents would, on occasion, buy her a banana or two—a great luxury and very expensive in pre-war Poland. More than once I got to the delicacies before they were fed to Roske, and, consequently, received appropriate punishment, including, I believe, spankings. Yes, my oldest sister, Baile, may she rest in peace, was tough.

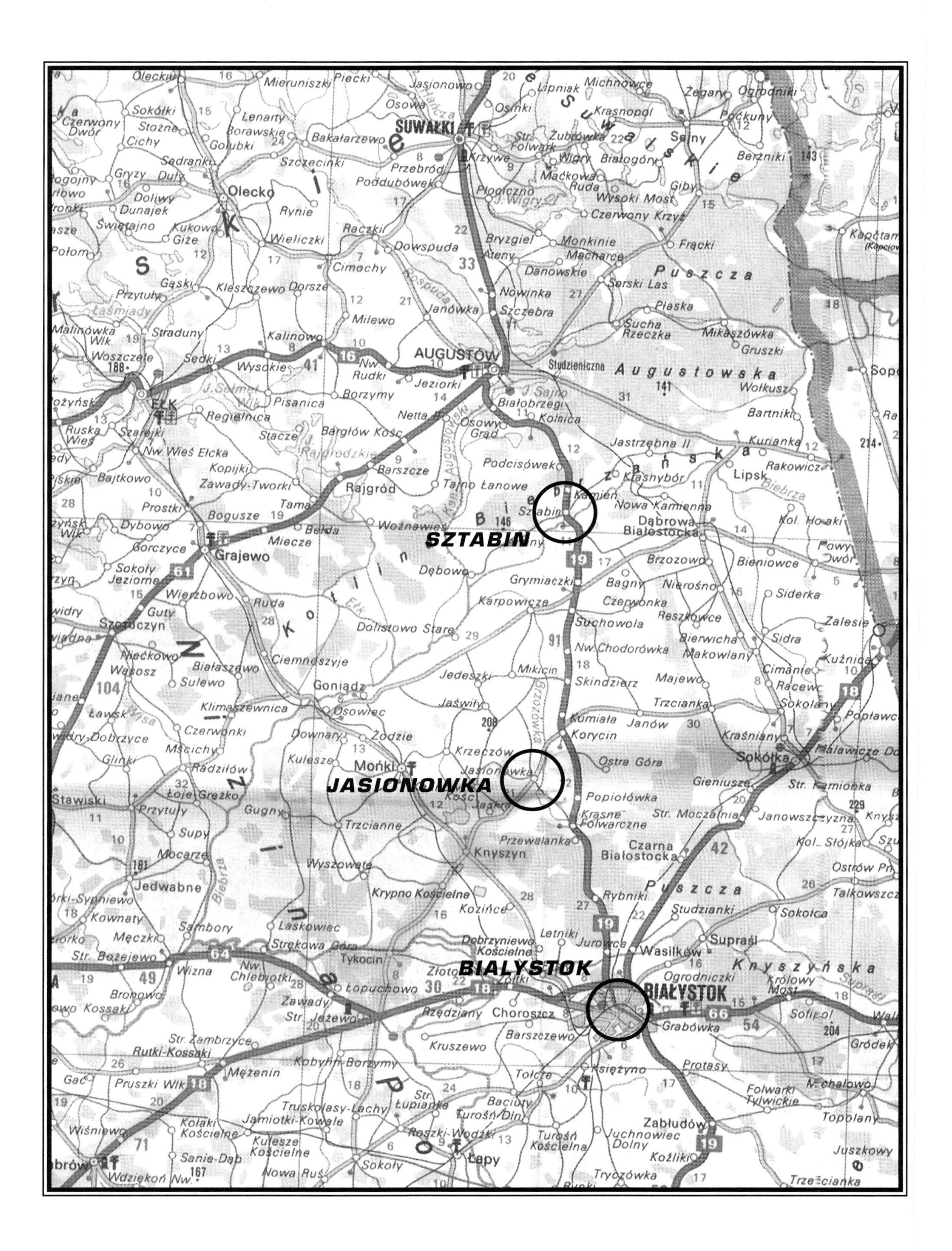
SZTABIN
JASIONOWKA
BIALYSTOK
SUWAŁKI
AUGUSTÓW
BIAŁYSTOK
Olecko
Ełk
Grajewo
Rajgród
Szczuczyn
Goniądz
Mońki
Knyszyn
Tykocin
Sokółka
Suchowola
Korycin
Dąbrowa Białostocka
Lipsk
Sejny
Choroszcz
Wasilków
Supraśl
Zabłudów
Łapy
Jedwabne
Wizna
Stawiski
Studzieniczna
Puszcza Augustowska
Puszcza Knyszyńska
Kotlina Biebrzańska
Pojezierze Suwalskie
Krasne Folwarczne
Czarna Białostocka
Szabin
Jasionówka
Kamień
Biebrza
Brzozówka

The town of Jasionowka was very small, like thousands of other towns in Eastern Europe. Some 2500 people lived in the town, and most of them were Jewish. The map on previous page shows where Jasionowka was in relation to Bialystok, the nearest large city, as well as to other towns in the area

Here is what Feitche had to say about Jasionowka in her diary:

> *The town of Jasionowka, located in the Bialystok Region of Poland about forty kilometers from the big city of Bialystok, was so small it was not even marked on the map. Of its two thousand inhabitants, fifteen hundred were Jews. Life was peaceful there. The marketplace stood quietly in the center of town with its church and a few Jewish shops. There were no special market days, no regular fairs. The people earned their living by hard, honest toil in this town known for its tanneries; one of them was famous throughout the country—the Skurdamik company which belonged to the Minski family. A supplier of leather for the Polish military, it was renowned for its high quality product. In addition, there were a number of smaller tanneries which worked for the private market and employed hundreds of people.*
>
> *Jasionowka was really far ahead of the surrounding towns in its productivity. The hide-scraps were used in other enterprises, such as glue factories, and there were shops for washing the animal-hair. Naturally, there was a Tanners Union, with its own long history. The Jewish and Polish workers lived together peacefully, with the same troubles and the same joys. Life proceeded normally. Every morning the factory whistles called Jews and Poles to their jobs. Together they celebrated the First of May. Together they went on strike. And together they rejoiced when the strike ended in victory.*

Jasionowka was far from beautiful, but it was picturesque, and to a child growing up there, it was the center of the universe and "home sweet home." The houses were small, old, and built of wood. The better ones had wooden floors, and others had no floors at all. Most houses had basements which could be reached by climbing down a wooden staircase. We had no electricity, no running water, no sewers, and no central heat. Firewood was used for cooking and heating. Producing firewood involved great effort and much energy, and bringing firewood from the outside into the house was a job most often assigned to young children. Most difficult of all, I think, was not having inside plumbing. We used an outhouse which was located some 100 feet from the house. During the long and cold winter months, that was no fun at all!

The hardest job in the world must have been being a wife and a mother of eight children in Jasionowka. My mother, may she rest in peace, worked like no other woman I have ever known. Imagine just preparing meals for a family of ten: potatoes by the bushel had to be peeled; noodles

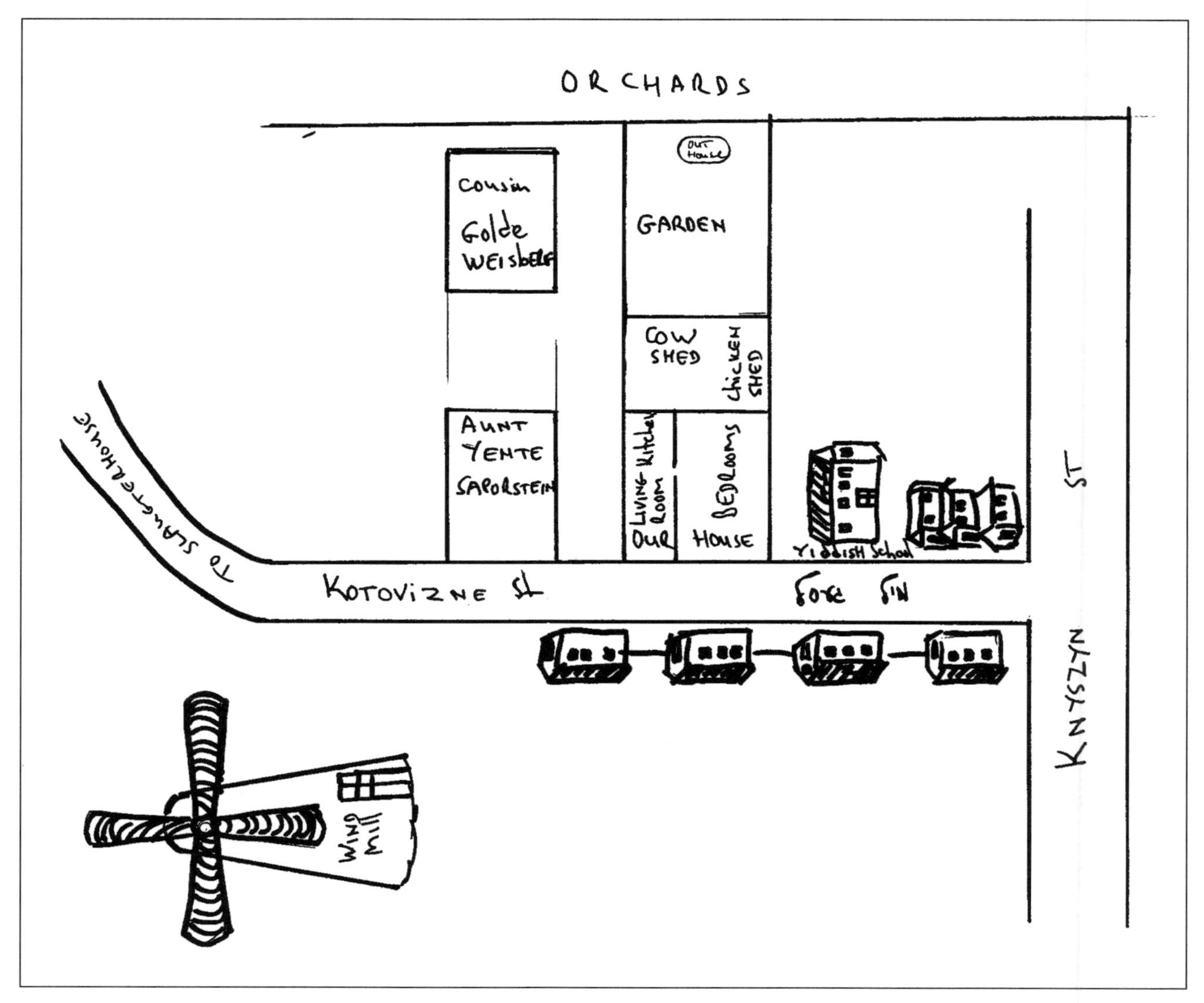

Our house on Kotovizue Street

had to be made from scratch; cows had to be milked; and sour cream, butter, and cheese had to be prepared at home. There were few stores where you could buy staples like sugar, salt, herring, and other essentials.

My mother also did laundry at home about once a month when garments, bedding, and other things had to be boiled, washed in a wooden tub called *baleiki*, and hung out to dry. Mending, sewing, and knitting were done by my mother with the help of my sisters. No wonder mothers were idealized and sung about in songs like "My Yiddishe Mame" and referred to as the greatest gift God has bestowed upon us.

When I was very young my parents lived in a small house located not far from the center of town on a street called Kotovizne or Mill Street. I will attempt to locate that little street and house on a sketch of the town as I remember it. The house was small. Attached to the house was a section where we kept a cow and chickens. In the back, we had a large garden, at the end of which was a wooden fence. In back of the fence a neighbor had an orchard and several trees—cherries, pears and apples. The trees had branches extending over the fence and onto our property. My brother Maishe and I often pulled down fruit with a special large stick and a hook made from a bent nail. I recall our neighbor chasing us and calling us thieves because we helped ourselves to delicious fruit, mostly within our air space. Fruit otherwise gotten never tasted so good.

I don't remember much about our old house, but I do remember enough to draw a sketch of the layout. Not far from our old house were fields that turned to mud in the fall and stayed that way until early summer. Passover was usually celebrated in the early spring. I and other children in the *shtetl* loved that time of the year. School would be dismissed weeks before Passover, and there was much to do. Every Jewish home received a thorough Passover (spring) cleaning. Preparing for Passover involved the young and old alike. *Matzah* baking was done in special "bakeries" set up for that purpose. Each family was assigned a day and time when they, their friends and their relatives, could come to roll the *matzot* to get them ready for the oven. Children were involved in the *matzah* baking events which went on around the clock. We, the youngsters, loved it.

With the cleaning done and the *matzah* baked, it was time to look forward to the actual holidays. On the day Passover was to start, the entire house was carefully inspected. All bread crumbs and other *chometz* were collected in a large wooden spoon, a piece of cloth was tied around it, and this was taken to a bonfire to be burned. Children old enough to do so were given the job of taking the wooden spoon to the bonfire.

There were no clothing stores in Jasionowka, and anything worn had to be made by a tailor or sewn at home. Shoes were made by shoemakers. Those who could afford it made sure that each member of the family was outfitted with new clothing for Passover. One suit and one pair of shoes normally had to last for a whole year.

I must have been four years old when my parents outfitted me in a beautiful new brown suit, white shirt and lovely new shoes for Passover. I could not wait to be all dressed up in my beautiful new outfit as I woke up the day Passover was to begin at sundown. Soon after breakfast I begged mother to let me dress up in my new outfit, and, in desperation, she gave in. Later, all dressed up, I went to take the wooden spoon with the *chometz* to the bonfire. When I got there, I found many of my friends playing in the field, and they asked me to join them. The ground was wet and slippery, and I fell again and again in the mud. With my new shoes and suit all muddy, I went home. It was then that I remember getting the first spanking I ever received from my father. I have never forgotten that; and you, Sarah, having heard that story many times, will never forget it either.

When I was about three or four years old, my parents purchased a house and tannery at the other end of town on a street known as Colonia. For me that place became home, and most of what I remember of Jasionowka I remember as a child growing up in that house. I loved it. I have drawn a sketch of our house, tannery, and related buildings which I believe is fairly accurate. In 1992 my brother Maishe, who now lives in Australia, went back to Poland to visit and spent half a day in Jasionowka. He tells me that our house and tannery are now changed beyond recognition. He gave me some photos which he took and which I will attach at the end of this book. They seem totally unfamiliar to me and certainly do not reflect the charm and beauty that place held for me while I was growing up.

The new house and tannery were purchased by my parents in the early 1930's. The family who sold this property to my parents used the funds from the sale to resettle in Argentina. I have often struggled with the question of why my parents did not leave Poland rather than buy the house and tannery. My parents certainly knew how difficult life in Poland was for Jews. Polish anti-Semitism was long-standing and deeply rooted in the culture. Although Jews had lived in Jasionowka since 1731, we were never fully accepted by our Polish neighbors, who looked upon us as strangers and resented our presence in their midst. We never fully assimilated into Polish society because the Poles did not allow us to do so. Poles, who were mostly Catholic, looked upon the Jews in their midst as Christ killers, as people who were to be blamed for all of their problems. Most Poles were illiterate, ignorant, and superstitious. They used the Jews as a convenient scapegoat that was easy to oppress. Polish governments, the kings and dictators, also promoted the hatred of Jews and blamed them for their own shortcomings. Even the Catholic Church, often led by drunken priests, sponsored and encouraged blind anti-Semitism. The ignorant masses didn't need much more encouragement.

A large percentage of the people in Jasionowka were, one way or the other, involved in producing leather and related products. We had one large leather factory owned and operated by the Minski family. That factory produced leather for the Polish army and employed, I believe, several hundred people. They even had their own generators producing electricity, the only electricity in town. They also had a manager who rode the first motorcycle in town. The Minski family lived in the center of town in the main square and were considered very wealthy. Because they were wealthy, the Soviets, who occupied our town in 1939, considered the Minskis a threat to society and deported them to a remote region of the Soviet Union known as Siberia. Because they were deported, most of the Minski family survived and several of them managed to move to Israel after the war where some of them still live.

The Minski factory was in a class by itself. There were probably six or eight other tanneries in Jasionowka, all of them small, employing 10 to 20 people, each producing one or several kinds of

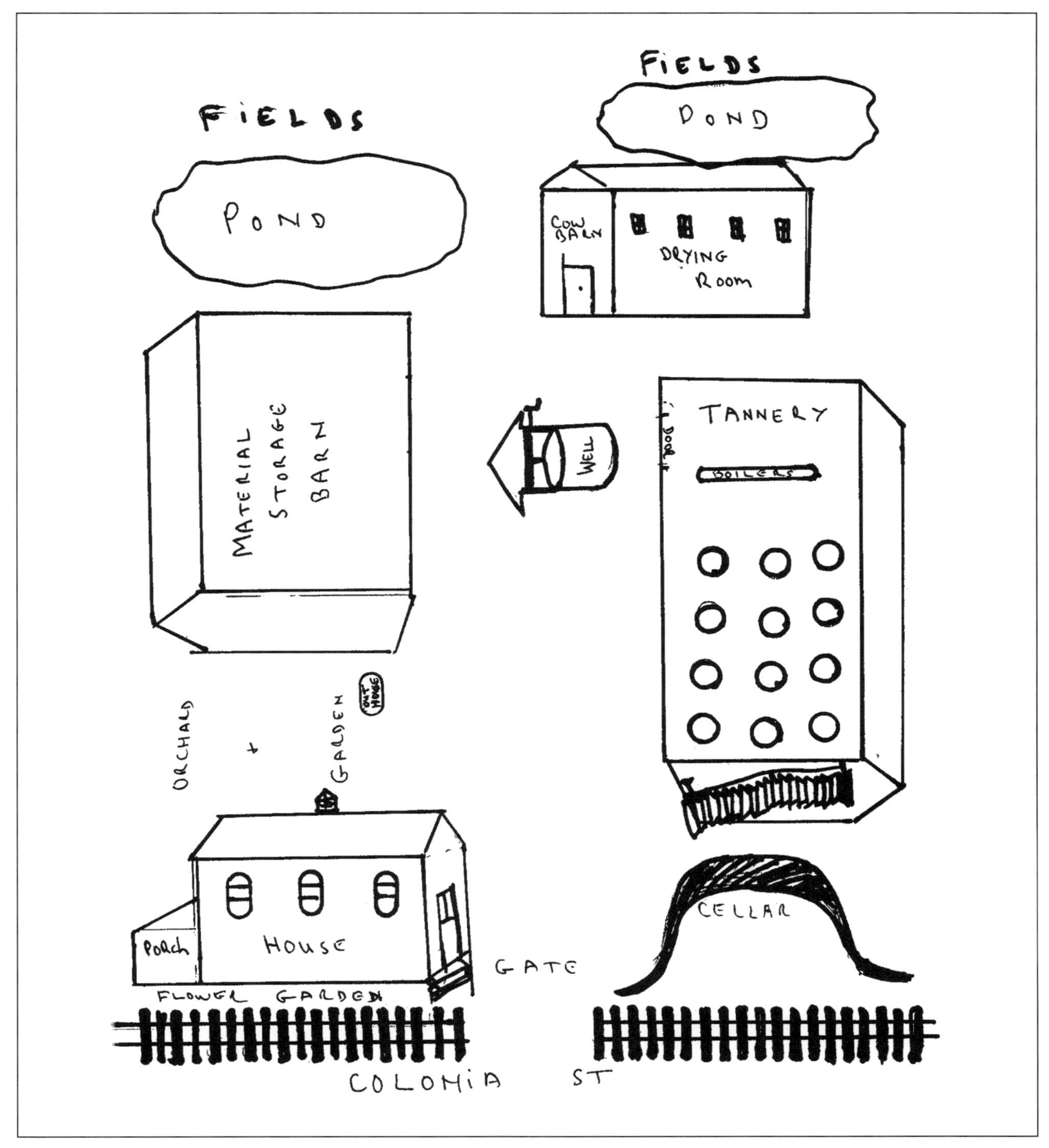

Our house and tannery on Colonia Street

leather. In addition, and related to the tanneries, there were several small factories making glue from hide by-products. One or two places washed and processed the hair from the hides which was later used to make winter boots, called *volaki,* and other hair products such as blankets. Also, since the process of making leather from hides required curing the hides in large vats by liberally sprinkling each hide with chopped-up oak bark, there were several "factories" drying and chopping the bark for sale to the tanneries.

Most of my family, including my father, his brother Mordche, Mordche's son, Shleime, etc., all owned tanneries and/or glue factories. Since it was very difficult to make a good living from a tannery, most male family members who were old enough ended up working in the tannery, often right after grammar school. Thus, in our family, my older brother, Maier, who was about twelve years older than I, and my other brother Maishe, who was only four years older than I, had already joined my father in the tannery before 1941. The work was terribly hard and quite dangerous since fumes from materials (lime) used to process the hides often produced gases which could make people sick or kill them. The work days were long and a week consisted of at least six long, hard days.

The major preoccupation of *shtetl* Jews was making a living, feeding and clothing their usually large families, and avoiding, as best they could, the hostile and often life threatening anti-Semitism. Religion played an important part in the lives of most Jews, as did culture and education. There was only one kind of religion in the *shtetl*, Orthodox. Nevertheless, within Orthodoxy, one could find those who were very Orthodox, praying no less than three times a day at one of the synagogues or at a *shtibl* (a room in a private house where members of a certain trade, e.g. tailors, gathered to pray). One could also find less religious Jews who went to the synagogue or *shul* only for Sabbath and holiday praying. Otherwise, they prayed at home on weekdays before going to work. When I was young, new winds of change blew over Eastern Europe. In Jasionowka secular movements (Zionism, bund) started to take root and weakened the traditional Orthodox domination of *shtetl* life.

Those who were traditional Orthodox did not send their children to Yiddish or Hebrew schools. Their sons were destined to get their traditional education in a *cheider*. When a boy was about four years old, the father would wrap the child in a *tallis* (prayer shawl) and carry the child to the *cheider* where the *rebbe* (teacher) would put a drop of honey on the first letter of the first page of the Five Books of Moses, and the boy would be allowed and encouraged to lick the honey off the page. This was the symbolic way of associating the love for Torah (learning) with sweetness. Often that association lasted a lifetime, as many of the boys went from *cheider* to *yeshiva* and spent the rest of their lives studying Torah.

We did not have a *yeshiva* in Jasionowka. Still, several weeks before Passover an entire *yeshiva*—students and teachers—moved to Jasionowka while their *yeshiva* was receiving a thorough cleaning in preparation for Passover. The students spent days and many nights studying in the synagogue. Each student was assigned families where they would receive meals. This was called

Esn Teg (To Eat Days). In my home we always had at least one *yeshiva* student for meals during that time of the year. For the most part, the students were bright and in many ways delightful young men, though fanatically religious. Often I would go to the synagogue to be with them. To this day I recall the first few words of a little song they often sang:

OLAM AZE	THIS WORLD
IS A SHMOLER BRIK	IS A NARROW BRIDGE
UN DERIKER, UN DERIKER	AND THE MAIN THING, AND THE MAIN THING
IS NISHT ZUM SHREREKN ZICH	IS NOT TO BE AFRAID

We, the youngsters of Jasionowka, always felt a void and were saddened when the students left our town and went back to their *yeshiva* for the holidays.

Because generations of Jews in *shtetlach* (towns) were isolated and had little mobility, they developed unique customs and traditions which dominated and influenced life from birth to death. Although they had little contact or connection with the non-Jewish world around them, they were in constant contact with their God whom they worshiped but also took to task. Tevya's "conversations" with God were typical.

So were those of the title character in I. L. Peretz's short story, "Berl the Tailor." It is the eve of Yom Kippur, and because Berl is not present in the synagogue, Levi-Yitzhok, the Rabbi of Berdichev, delays the Kol Nidre chant. He sends the *shammes* to summon Berl. Berl comes and tells the Rabbi that he refuses to pray to a God who has punished him for taking what is rightfully his by custom, fox pelts left over from a coat he had made for a Polish nobleman. God, he says, is unfair. He explains the details to the Rabbi and asks, "Am I right, Rabbi?" Rabbi Levi-Yitzhok says, "Yes, and if you stand fast, they will have to give in to you." The Rabbi turns back to the ark, looks up at the heavens, listens for a few minutes, and then turns toward Berl. "You have prevailed, Berl," he says. "Go home and get your *kittl* and your *tallit*."

Let me give you a little history, a child's version, very much abbreviated:

WHEN THE JEWISH PEOPLE LIVED IN ISRAEL (PALESTINE) IN BIBLICAL DAYS, THEY WERE OFTEN SUBJECTED TO THREATS OF INVASIONS, WARS, AND ON SEVERAL OCCASIONS, EXPULSIONS. AFTER THE DESTRUCTION OF THE SECOND TEMPLE IN 70 C.E., JEWS WERE DISPERSED, AND SOME ENDED UP IN SPAIN AND OTHER PLACES. THOSE WHO SETTLED IN SPAIN LIVED THERE FOR QUITE A WHILE AND ACTUALLY ENJOYED A GOLDEN CULTURAL PERIOD. HOWEVER, THEY WERE EXPELLED FROM SPAIN AT APPROXIMATELY THE SAME TIME COLUMBUS SAILED ON his voyage to America in 1492. Expelled from Spain, Jews moved on eastward through central Europe, and many landed in Germany. There, they invented the Yiddish language by borrowing from the old German dialect which became the basis of about 70% of Yiddish. Where there was not a German word they could use, they would use a Hebrew word. And inevitably, in each country where Yiddish was spoken, they added some words from the language of that country. For instance, in Poland the word for floor was *podloga*, which was borrowed from the Polish language.

After a while Jewish people were driven further east, and many ended up in Poland. Some Jews actually settled in Poland as early as the 13th century. In 1264, a Polish king known as Boleslaw the Pious granted a charter of protection to the Jewish people in order to induce them to settle in Poland. At that time Poland was terribly backwards without industry or commerce, and the king hoped that the Jewish settlers would help develop and enrich Poland.

Poland underwent a number of divisions, reunifications, and more divisions, and many Jews ended up under either Austria-Hungarian, Prussian, or Russian control. Thus that area became known as the Pale of Settlement.

Although Jews were invited to settle in Poland and welcomed initially, it did not take long before their presence was resented and blind anti-Semitism resurfaced. Jews were prohibited from owning agricultural land, their economic freedoms were restricted, and their lives became anything but pleasant for years to come.

According to an article published in 1978 in a magazine called *Bialystoker Shtime*, Jews settled in Jasionowka in 1731. In the year 1800, 393 Jews lived in Jasionowka. It is very likely that my own family were among the first settlers in Jasionowka. Whenever I would ask my father where we had come from, he would always tell me, Jasionowka. His parents lived there, and his grandparents lived there, and that was all he knew.

Jasionowka, like all other towns, was a tight little community, mostly Jewish, surrounded by Polish farmers. In the town, life became well defined and regimented. People knew their place and knew what to expect. Mobility was minimal. Most people were born, grew up, and lived all their adult lives in the same town, where they eventually died and were buried in centuries-old cemeteries.

My mother was born in a town called Sztabin. It was located about 40 miles north of Jasionowka. During World War I, Sztabin was destroyed by fire, and not many Jews lived there after World War I. As a little boy, I visited Sztabin several times but can remember little about it. I do know that my grandparents lived in a house on the banks of a large river and were involved in some cattle trading.

Of the six children in my mother's family, three of them — Dora Meltzer, Mary Kaufman, and Irving Meyers — immigrated to the United States at a very young age and settled in Rochester, New York. They left Sztabin in order to escape poverty and anti-Semitism and to seek a better life in the *Goldene Medine* (Golden Land). Both my maternal grandparents died before World War II began, and unfortunately I don't remember much about them.

What I do remember is that my parents often talked about their wedding and the three days it took them to travel from Sztabin to Jasionowka by horse-drawn wagon with frequent stops for drinks, more drinks and merriment. Because my family had lived in Jasionowka for a very long time, we were related to many people in Jasionowka. I have attached a short version of a family tree which will show that my grandfather and grandmother, Moshe and Mariashe Schuster, had eight children, most of whom lived in Jasionowka, although eventually their children ended up in many parts of the world.

My uncle Irving Meyers, his wife Minnie, Jane & I and my aunt Dora Meltzer taken at our wedding in 1955.

Since my aunts and uncles had anywhere from six to ten children, it is not difficult to see why I had such a large number of aunts, uncles, cousins and other relatives living nearby. The family photo (next page) with about 48 people is not complete. It was taken about 1920, some seven or eight years before I was born. My parents and only five of their eight children are in this picture.

Tradition and custom required that a family provide a dowry to a daughter and her husband. Often it was part of the "contract" negotiated by the matchmaker and the two families involved. A family that could not provide an appropriate dowry was often unable to arrange a marriage for their daughter. This heavy burden was reflected in a song called "Drei Techterlach-Three Daughters." My parents, who had five daughters, worried much, and my father often sang that song with tears in his eyes. I have set forth the text to this song in Yiddish and in my own rough translation.

THREE DAUGHTERS

WHEN WITH GOD'S HELP AND
GOOD FORTUNE, WE SHALL MARRY
OFF OUR OLDEST DAUGHTER,
I SHALL DANCE AND MUCH REJOICE
WITH A CLEAR AND HAPPY VOICE.
PLAY MUSICIANS, PLAY SOMEHOW
THE OLDEST CHILD IS MARRIED NOW;
LEFT WE ARE WITH SEVERAL MORE
STILL MUCH BETTER THAN BEFORE.

WHEN I WILL SEE MY SECOND DAUGHTER
DRESSED IN HER WHITE WEDDING GOWN,
I WILL DANCE, REJOICE, AND JEST -
ANOTHER STONE ROLLED OFF MY CHEST;
PLAY MUSICIANS, ON AND ON
OUR SECOND DAUGHTER NOW IS GONE;
NOW REMAINS THE YOUNGEST ONE
WITH GOD'S HELP SHE WILL BE GONE.

WHEN THE LAST ONE'S CHANCE WILL COME
I WILL BE THERE SAD & NUMB;
THE YOUNGEST CHILD IS GOING NOW-
TEARS REPLACE THE JOY SOMEHOW;
PLAY MUSICIANS, ON AND ON
ALL OUR CHILDREN NOW ARE GONE;
HARD IT WAS WITH DAUGHTER THREE
NOW WITHOUT THEM WOE IS ME.

DRAY TECHTERLACH

Van mit maz'l, glik un leb'n
Dos ershte techter'l ich vel oysgeb'n
Oy, vel ich tants'n, hop hop hop,
Arop a yoch fun kop.

Shpilt, klezmorem, oy a leb'n
Dos ershte techter'l haynt oys-gegeb'n,
'Siz mir geblib'n nor techter tsvey,
Vi halt men shoyn ba zey.

Shpilt, klezmorem, oy nemt di fidl,
Un gicher shpilt mir oys a freylich lidl,
Unzer simche veyst nor eyn Got
Un der vos techter hot. (2X)

Ven ich vel zen dos tsveyte meydl
Ongeton in vays'n chupe kleydl,
Oy, vel ich trink'n, a tents'l geyn,
Arop fun harts a shteyn.
Oy, vel ich trink'n oy vel ich trink'n,
Arop fun harts a shteyn.
Shpilt klezmorem, oy a leb'n
Dos tsveyte techter'l haynt oysgegeb'n;
Dos mezinkele geblib'n mir,
Vi halt men shoyn ba yir.

Shpilt, klezmorem, far mechetonim,
Zol'n naches hob'n oyoh kaptsonim,
A kind oys-geb'n, Gotenyu,
A meydl nooh dertsu. (2X)

Ven bam letst'n 'chvel shpil'n her'n
Vel ich epis shteyn un troyerik zler'n:
Dos letste techter'l shoyn oych avek,
Un vos iz noch der tsvek.
'Sletste techter'l, 'sletste techter'l,
Un vos iz noch der tsvek.

Shpilt, klezmorem, aroys mit trer'n,
Dos letste bet'l vet haynt leydik ver'n
Dos gentse shtib'l, ir kleyder shaynk,
Oy 'stut mir vey, un baynk.

Shpilt, klezmorem, bazetst di kale,
Tsugenum'n ba mir di kinder ale,
Dray techter iz a shverer yoch,
Nor on zey iz shverer noch. (2X)

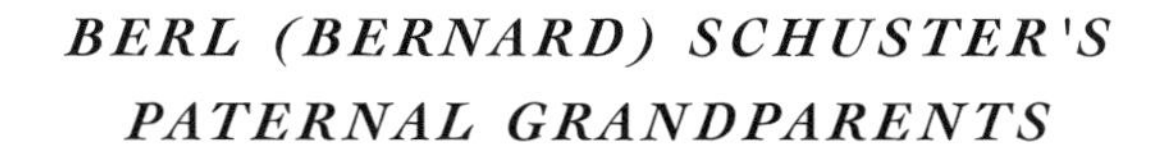

BERL (BERNARD) SCHUSTER'S PATERNAL GRANDPARENTS

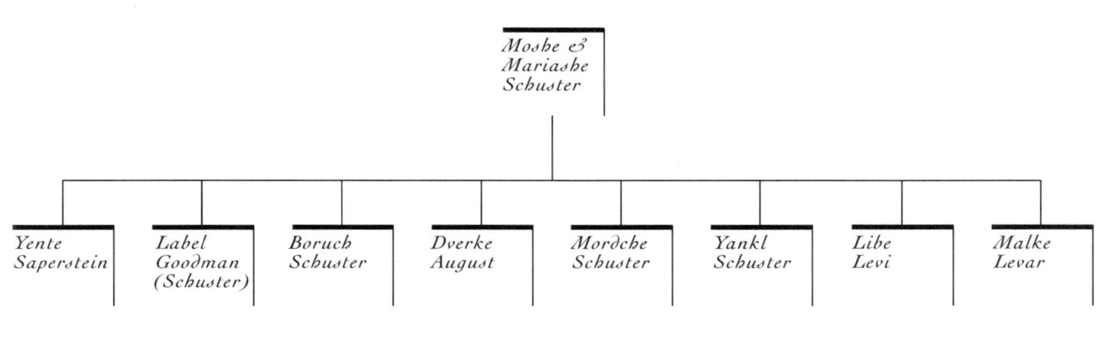

BERL (BERNARD) SCHUSTER'S MATERNAL GRANDPARENTS

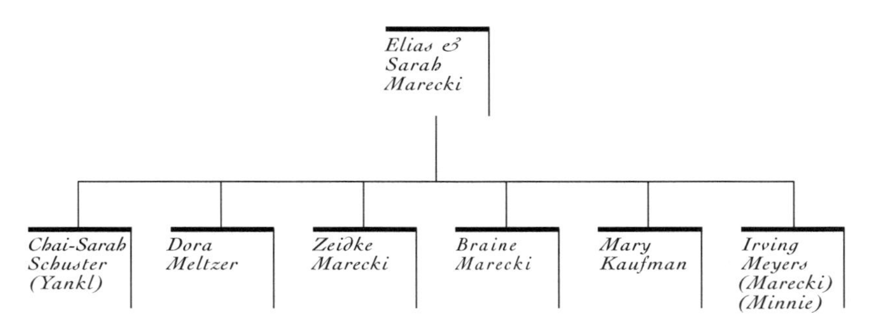

BERL (BERNARD) SCHUSTER'S FAMILY TREE

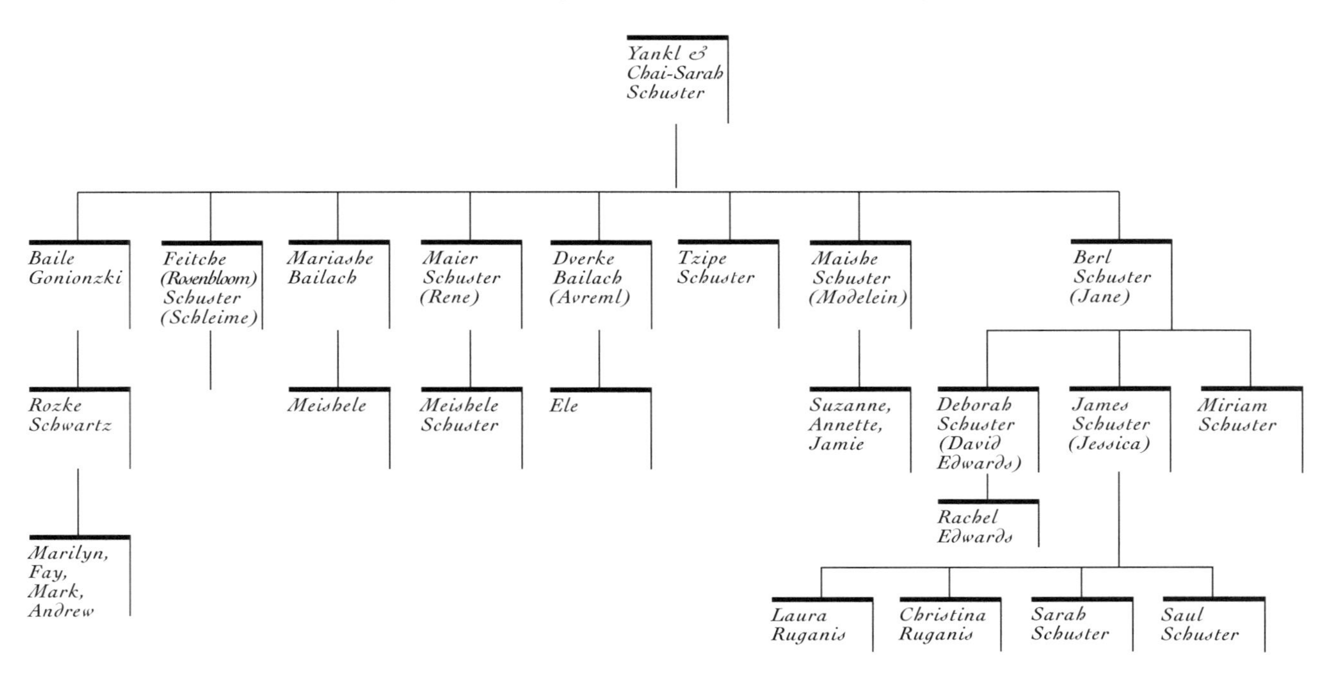

Schuster Family Photo (1920)

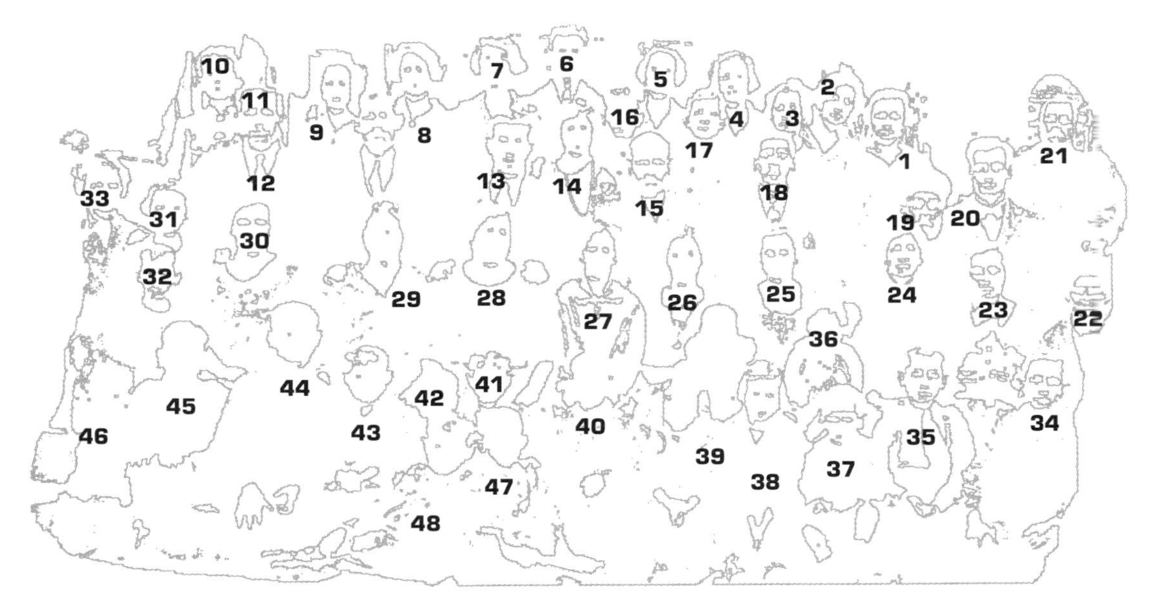

As best I can recall, these are the names of the people in the photograph:

1. *Freidke Saperstein (cousin)*
2. *Willia Movski*
3. *Bailke Saperstein (cousin; child of Yente Saperstein [#24]. She grew up in a house next to our house on Kotovizne Street and later emigrated to Ireland and married a Rabbi. Some years ago, Bailke came to visit us and brought us a* shabbat challah *cover she had embroidered. It is a precious object Jamie and Jessica Shcuster and their family now use every Friday night.)*
4. *Dvora Schuster (cousin)*
5. *Zlatke Saperstein (Cooperman) (cousin; child of Yente Saperstein.) She and her large family lived in England and eventually moved to Israel where they are prominent in many fields of endeavor.*
6. *Shleime Schuster (cousin; son of my uncle Mordche Schuster [#12]. He was married to Ite Schuster [#9] with whom he had three children. After losing his wife and the children in the Holocaust, he married my sister Feitche. He played an important part in the life of our shtetl both before and during the Holocaust. In many ways, he was the patriarch of our family. He and my sister lived in Guadalajara, Mexico, after the war. He moved to Israel after my sister died. He died on April 1, 1994.*
7. *Baile Schuster (sister)*
8. *Zlatke Schuster (Zlotorinsky) (cousin; 2nd oldest child of Mordche Schuster [#12]. She lives in Guadalajara and was also my Godmother.)*
9. *Ite Schuster (was married to Shleime Schuster [#6]*
10. *Solie Schuster*
11. *Yankl Schuster (father)*
12. *Mordche Schuster (my father's brother)*
13. *Leibl Goodman (He changed his name from Schuster to Goodman after moving to England.)*
14. *Fannie Goodman*
15. *Berl Levar (husband of my aunt Malke Levar [#26]; he was a coachman [*balegole *in Yiddish].)*
16. *Dovid*
17. *Avreml*
18. *Hochem Weisberg*
19. *Itche Saperstein*
20. *Hochum Beilach*
21. *Relative from Iavne*
22. *Mother of Aunt*
23. *Chaie Leibe Beilach*
24. *Yente Saperstein (the oldest of my father's sisters; lived with her family in a little house next to our house on Kotovizne Street)*
25. *Golde Weisberg*
26. *Malke Levar (youngest of my father's sisters; married to Berl Levar [#15])*
27. *Chane Foigl Schuster*
28. *Mary Goodman*
29. *Itke Schuster (wife of my uncle Mordche Schuster [#12])*
30. *Chaye Sarah Schuster (mother)*
31. *Mariashe Schuster (sister)*
32. *Dverke Schuster (sister)*
33. *Feitche Schuster (sister)*
34. *Freidke Schuster (third oldest child of Mordche Schuster; died in France; survived by a daughter, Sesil Kristal)*
35. *Yosl Schuster*
36. *Avreml Saperstein (youngest son of my aunt Yente Saperstein [#24])*
37. *Avreml Weisberg (son of Golde Weisberg [#25]; grandson of Yente Saperstein [#24]. He survived the war, moved to Israel, and was known as Levani.)*
38. *Chaye Levar*
39. *Mariashe Levar*
40. *Menashe Schuster (son of my uncle Baruch Schuster. He emigrated to Palestine before the war and was a soldier in the British army. He came to visit us in Jasionowka in 1939 just before the war broke out. His wife, Frieda, and children live in Israel.)*
41. *Mariashe Schuster (cousin)*
42. *Maishe Shuster (youngest son of my uncle Mordche Schuster; he and his wife Esther live in Mexico City.)*
43. *Chane Schuster*
44. *Elie Chaim Schuster (son of my uncle Mordche Schuster. He survived the Holocaust and went to Guadalajara. He and his family lived in a house that had a common wall with the house lived in by his brother Shloime [#6] and Shloime's wife, my sister Feitche [#33]. After Elie Chaim died, his wife, Teibl, and their three children moved to Mexico City where they now live.)*
45. *Maier Schuster (brother)*
46. *Tzipe Schuster (sister)*
47. *Yudl Schuster*
48. *Meyer Levar*

For centuries *shtetl* life was stagnant and moved at a very slow pace. Change was gradual and hardly noticeable. Most people knew their place in the community and by-and-large were satisfied.

A typical *shtetl* was governed by a *Kahal* (town council), the central authority. On a grassroots level, the *shtetl* was run by *Khevres* (voluntary associations organized around work, study, or charitable functions). Among other things they would visit the sick, help the poor, welcome visitors, and provide dowries for poor young women to help them get married.

There were a number of institutions around which *shtetl* life was organized. Of course, the most important one was the family. The others typically included:

- The ***shul*** or synagogue. To a significant extent, life in the *shtetl* revolved around the *shul*. It was not just a place of worship. It was a meeting place, a house of learning, a shelter for the poor, and much more.

- The ***mikvah*** or ritual bath house. The *mikvah* was used for religious and hygienic purposes by both men and women.

- The ***cheider*** or school. The *cheider* was where little boys studied with a teacher known as the *Rebbe* or *Melamed*.

- The ***yeshiva*** or Talmudic academy. This was where older boys continued their religious studies, often in preparation for becoming a rabbi.

- The ***mark*** or marketplace. Several times a year an outdoor market or *yerid* was set up for the exchange of goods and services. Non-Jews, too, gathered at the *mark*, and on occasion a pogrom developed.

- The ***besoylem*** or cemetery. The *besoylem* also served as an archive, a source of family and town history.

The ***shtetl*** was home to a number of individuals who played important roles:

- The ***Rabbi***, the town's spiritual leader. Some *Rabbis* became famous, like the Rabbi of Berdichev. In most towns the *Rabbi* led prayer services, ruled on questions of *kashrut*, and arbitrated disputes.

- The ***Chazan*** or cantor. The *Chazan* led the musical portion of the services and greatly enhanced the lives of *shtetl* Jews. As a boy, I sang in a choir with the *chazan* of our *shul*.

- The ***Melamed*** or ***Rebbe***. The *Melamed* or *Rebbe* was the teacher. He taught young boys to read the prayer book and other related studies. Ask anyone who grew up in a *shtetl* which *shtetl* character played a significant part in his development, and he will probably name the *Melamed* or *Rebbe*. Often, unfit to make a living any other way, the *Melamed* labored to teach little boys their Hebrew letters and prayers, using strict discipline in lieu of pedagogic skills. In Jasionowka the *Melamed* was known as *Yad Echad* (one arm). This did not prevent him from holding a leather belt in his remaining hand and using it to discipline.

- The ***shohet/mohel***. The *shohet* performed the ritual slaughtering of animals for kosher meat and often was the person who performed circumcisions.

- The ***shammes***. The *shammes* was the caretaker of the *shul*.

- The ***badchen***. Not every *shtetl* had a *badchen*, but no Jewish wedding was complete without one. The *badchen*, acting as master of ceremonies, would entertain and preach. Often he made the bride and her parents laugh and cry by playing on their emotions. He would give advice to the bride and groom, warning the bride of the perils of having a mother-in-law, and pleading with the mother-in-law to be kind and understanding.

Most towns had a strict social structure that regarded inhabitants as either *Sheine Yiden* (beautiful Jews) or *Proste Yiden* (plain Jews). However, being a *Sheine Yid* had nothing to do with being physically beautiful. The rabbi, scribe, and teacher were *Sheine Yiden*. A tradesmen or plain workman was a *Proste Yid*. Learning made the difference.

Secular life revolved around the market square, where many of the shops were located. In Jasionowka the market square also accommodated the secular school (*Tarbut* School) and the Christian Church. The sketch which follows on the next page reflects, as best as I can remember, the layout of the market square.

I remember our school house, a one-story building facing the square. In the building were classrooms where teaching was going on. The school was located between the priest's estate to the left and the Catholic Church several hundred feet to the right. Between the school and the church were a number of shops and houses. The building closest to the school contained a hat making shop, as well as the hat-maker's large family, the Berman family.

My recollection of my early school years are faded and blurred. I do recall the long walks which I had to and from school, since my family lived far away from the center of town, a walk of perhaps a mile or two each way. Often I would spend after school time at my sister Feitche's house, since after my parents bought the house and tannery on Colonia Street, our old house was given to Feitche and her husband. This house therefore became a second home for me. Feitche's house on Kotovizne Street was just a five minute walk from school. Since this was the house I was born in, it had special meaning for me. Most of my friends lived in that neighborhood, as did many of my relatives.

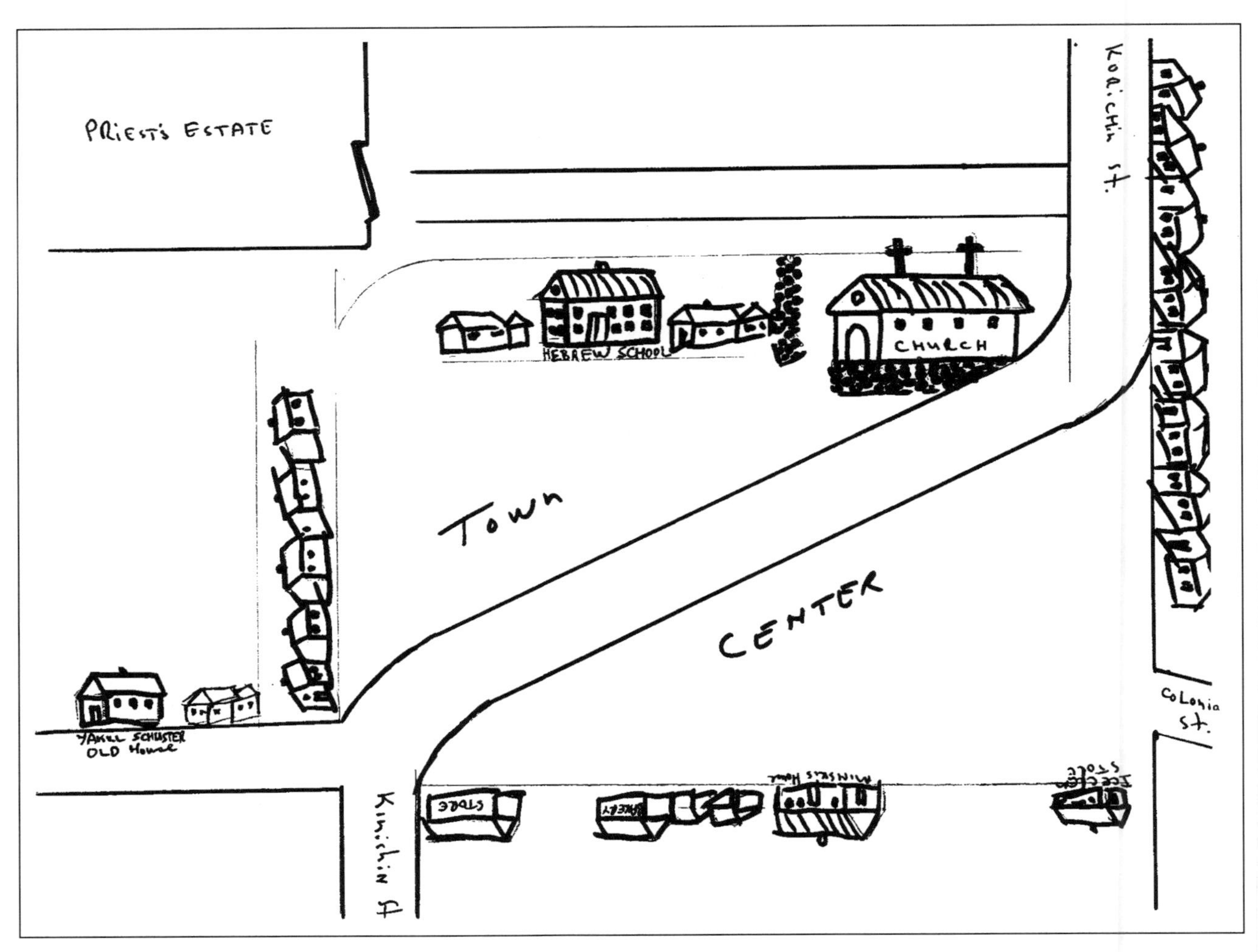

Market Square in Jasionowka

Across the square from my school was a bakery where for several *groshen* (pennies) you could buy the best *kuchen* (sweet buns) in the world. This made the long walks to school almost worthwhile. If you should question whether the Jasionowka sweet buns were in fact the best in the world, let me tell you that a piece of black bread with sugar sprinkled on it was also ambrosia to a young boy of four or five in Jasionowka. The adults preferred a piece of black bread with rendered goose fat spread on it.

As a young student, I was far from outstanding. Most of the time I would sketch and draw rather than concentrate on the subjects being taught. This was particularly true in a class being taught by a pretty young woman, with whom I was very much in love. The fact that I was eight or nine years old and she was in her twenties did not bother me. Day after day I would sketch her beautiful face in a special notebook I kept for that project. One day she walked to the back of the classroom and came to stand in back of me without my being aware of her presence. After class she asked me to remain and asked to see my sketch book. She looked through it, took me in her arms, kissed me, and asked if she could keep the book. This was a high point in my school life and left a lasting imprint on my memory. Sadly, at the end of the summer, this teacher whom I loved took her own life because the man she loved, the manager of Minski's leather factory, had betrayed her. I was very sad and heartbroken.

In school, the main language was Hebrew. We also studied Polish. Yiddish was spoken at home and in the streets. School was lots of fun. We played games both in and out of the school building. We also played tricks on our teachers, such as spreading some glue on a teacher's chair just before the teacher we did not like was about to come in and sit down.

In Jasionowka, as in all other small towns, the Jews were isolated and had little contact with non-Jews. As a result of this isolation, Jews in town interacted with each other so closely that it was almost like a large, extended family. Thus, a family event (for example, a wedding) became a town event. Joys and sorrows were shared by all. Community affiliation was so strong that even after immigrating to America, Jews from a *shtetl* sought each other out and formed *landsmen* associations with close ties.

Thus, despite the outside hostility, life in the *shtetl* was in many ways very sweet. Childhood was mostly happy and secure. I still remember the love I received from my parents and older sisters and brothers. I was never lonely in pre-war Jasionowka. To this day, I remember my brother Maier carrying me on his shoulders to the little library where he would read books to me and teach me how to play chess. I remember my brother Maishe teaching me how to make ice skates by carving wood into the shape of a skate to which a steel edge was attached. The steel edge was made from an instrument like a scythe used in the tannery for removing imperfections from the hide.

Four of my sisters, and one brother, were married while I was a small boy. I will never forget the love I received from my sisters, their boyfriends and husbands. During the summer, they would take me for hikes in the forests around Jasionowka, where we would pick blueberries, mushrooms, flowers, and plants of various sorts. They helped me explore the universe, taught me to love nature and all living things. These were lessons I have never forgotten.

Feeding a large family was never easy. We had little money and few stores to buy things in. Consequently, most women became excellent cooks by using their ingenuity. The most common foods were bread and potatoes. Those who could afford it also had fish and meat, at least for *Shabbat*.

I can't recall all the dishes my mother created from potatoes, probably several dozen dishes. Boiled potatoes, mashed potatoes, several kinds of potato *kugels*, potato *knishes*, potato soups, and on Saturday night, *peltzlach*, potatoes boiled in their skins and eaten with fried onions and oil.

Often there were neighbors and friends who gathered around our large table on Saturday night to eat potato *peltzlach* with us and to discuss the latest news from the outside world as well as town gossip.

Potatoes—in Yiddish, *bulves*—played such an important part in our lives that we even had a little song about *bulves*:

ZUNTIK BULVES	SUNDAY POTATOES
MONTIC BULVES	MONDAY POTATOES
DINSTICK, MITVOCH BULVES	TUESDAY, WEDNESDAY POTATOES
DONERSCHTICK BULVES	THURSDAY POTATOES
FRITICK BULVES	FRIDAY POTATOES
SHABES VIDER BULVES	SATURDAY AGAIN POTATOES

I have been asked where all those potatoes came from and how we kept potatoes without refrigeration. I have drawn a sketch of a very special cellar we had next to our house where potatoes stayed without spoiling for almost the entire year. We also kept other fruits and vegetables (carrots, beets, apples, pears, etc.) in that cellar, as well as milk, sour cream, cheese, and other dairy products.

The cellar was constructed partly below and mostly above ground by forming a thick reinforced concrete structure and covering it with several feet of earth. You entered the cellar by one door which you closed before opening a second door, thereby keeping heat and light out. The structure had a small window on each side which was covered so no light could penetrate. We purchased potatoes from farmers who delivered horse-drawn wagon loads of freshly dug potatoes and sent them down a chute through the little windows into large bins in the cellar. Often we and our friends would help the farmers dig potatoes and collect them in large sacks for delivery to us.

The cellar structure was a wonderful place to play. I used to sit with my dog Finka on top of the cellar for hours waiting for something to happen in the street below. It was our favorite outpost. Finka was "my" dog, large, pure white, and very loving. I believe this breed of dogs originated in Finland and was well-suited to cold winter weather. Finka slept with me and followed me around whenever I was at home. On occasion, he followed me to school and waited for me until school was out. Finka died of old age about 1940 and we, the children, gave him a proper funeral by placing his body in a grave in our garden underneath an apple tree. The loss of Finka was overwhelming to me and foretold of the much greater losses that were to follow.

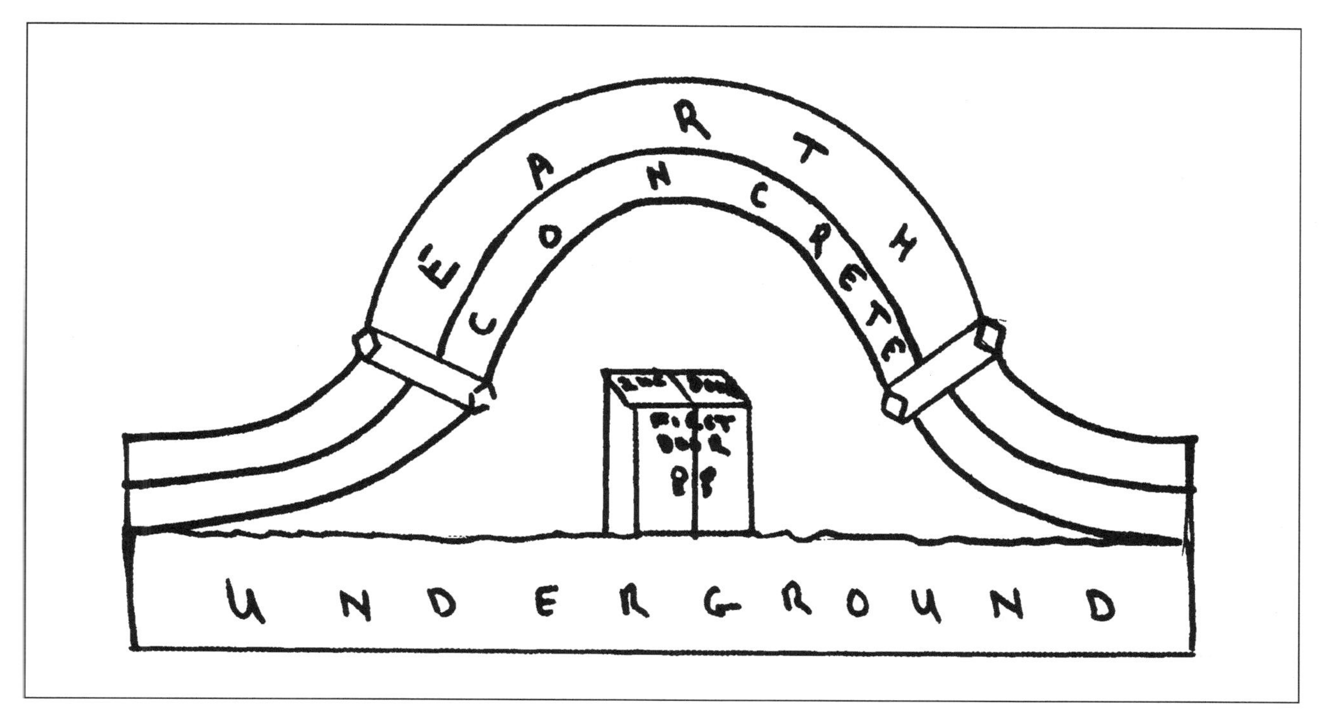

Side view of our cellar.

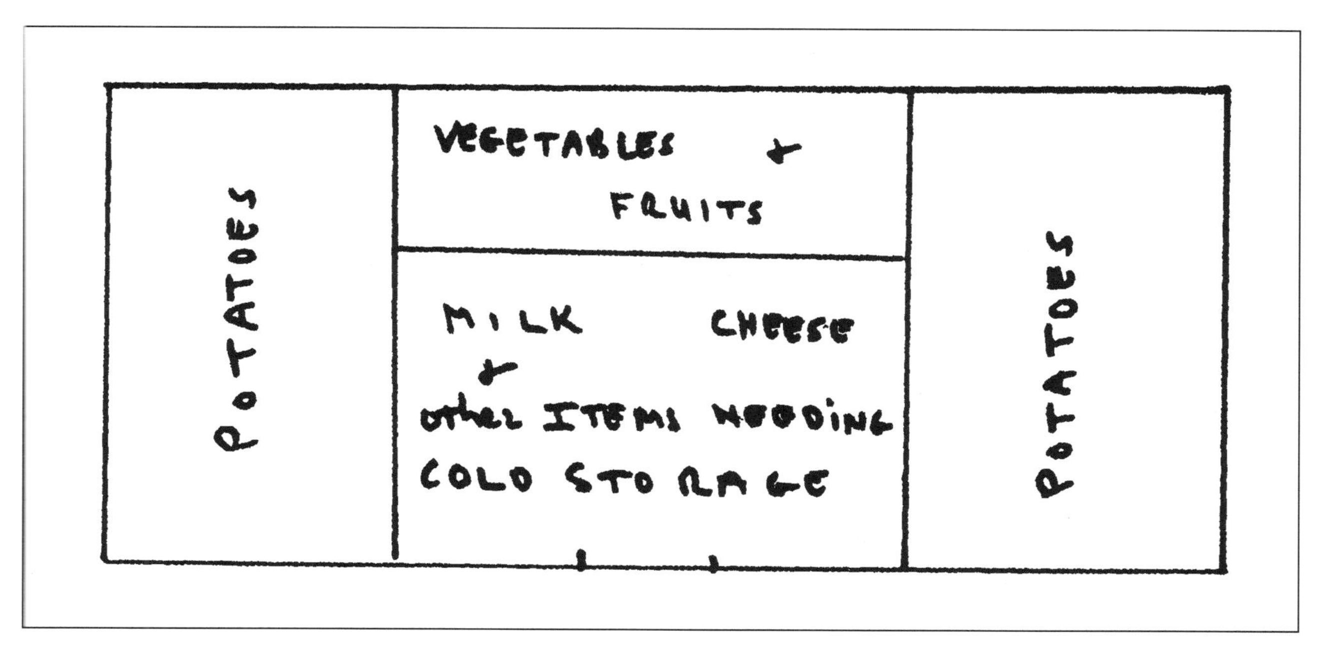

Floor view of our cellar.

In Jasionowka we also had a community cellar located in the center of town near the wooden synagogue, known as a *lodovnie* (ice house). In the middle of winter the *lodovnie* was filled with cut ice blocks covered with straw kept frozen for use during the summer months. If someone in the *shtetl* were sick and needed ice, it was provided. Butcher shops all received ice during the summer months to keep meat from spoiling.

I believe the security and love given me by my family before the war gave me the strength to survive the terrible times that followed.

In 1939, when I was just eleven years old, traditional life in Jasionowka changed drastically. The well-defined customs, traditions, and aspects of life in the *shtetl* were turned upside down and changed beyond recognition by the ill winds that came with World War II.

On September 1, 1939 Germany attacked Poland. The corrupt Polish government was too weak to resist the modern German Army and its Blitzkrieg. It took just a few days for the mechanized German army to destroy the Polish army which had had to fight German tanks and planes with soldiers on horseback.

The German army marched into Jasionowka about one week after they attacked Poland. They announced that, due to a pact Germany had made with the Soviet Union, our area of Poland would now become part of the Soviet Union, and the German army would withdraw. The Jewish people rejoiced.

Life under Soviet occupation was an improvement over life in pre-occupied Poland. Our Hebrew school was changed to a Soviet style ten-year school. I suddenly blossomed and became an excellent student. This allowed me to join the Pioneers, and I was elected President of the Young Pioneers at our school. At age eleven, I was suddenly a leader of boys and girls, wearing a red scarf and Pioneer pin, and proud of it.

Because my father owned a tannery and had employees, he was considered by the Soviets as a wealthy exploiter of the proletariat and a prospect for deportation. As it turned out, we were not deported, and that turned out to be most unfortunate. Had we been deported to Siberia, chances are most of our family would have survived.

While I was enjoying school and extra curricular activities, my family closely followed news about the war and Hitler's triumphs in Europe. My parents often talked about the danger we were in but could think of no way out. Travel out of Soviet-occupied Poland was not feasible, and Hitler's army was much too close for comfort.

My family in happier times (1938).

My brother Maier on ground, my sister Feitche and her future husband Avreml Rosenbloom, seated, Yankele Kliminsky, a cousin and my mother's brother, Zeideke, at top.

Rena with her husband—my brother Maier.

My sister Mariashe and her husband, Chaim Beilach.

My cousin Maishe Shuster, who lives in Mexico, upper row, second from right. My sister Dverke, lower right, with her classmates.

MY CHILDHOOD ENDS ABRUPTLY—GERMAN OCCUPATION BEGINS

Without warning, on Sunday, June 21, 1941, the German self-proclaimed superman struck again. That Sunday was a beautiful, sunny day. My niece, Roske, and I had gone to the fields in back of our house and tannery to play and to pick flowers. We were carefree. Suddenly we heard the noise of airplanes and saw dozens of planes coming in low over the horizon headed in the direction of our town. Within minutes bombs were falling and exploding not very far from where we were. Roske and I, scared to death, ran home to find out that the German planes were attacking the Minski Tanneries. War had caught up with us once again. A dark shadow had fallen over us and all of Europe, and we knew then that this was the beginning of the end for life as we knew it.

Feitche's words:

The town is sunk in gloom. From time to time, tattered remnants of the Soviet armed forces pass through the area. Some of them try to allay our fears: the Germans will never reach our town, they will be driven back before they ever get here. But the disorder of the Red Army is demoralizing. They seem to have fallen apart. They themselves are at a loss as to which way to go. One thing everyone agrees on—there must have been a betrayal by certain Soviet leaders.

But that knowledge doesn't help our situation here. Quite the contrary. Everyone knows a horrible time is near. More than one of us will die. (It never occurred to us that almost everyone would die.) The mood is oppressive. Faces darken. From day to day, things grow worse. The German army is advancing relentlessly. Occasionally an isolated Soviet automobile drives by, but actually, where can it go, when their army is encircled?

The general morale in Jasionowka sinks lower and lower. Soon the most corrupt elements among the Poles sense the defenselessness of the Jews. They don't even wait for the Germans to arrive. They are already coming in from the villages, breaking into Jewish homes, looting in broad daylight, destroying whatever they cannot carry away with them. (They felt at once that they now had powerful support: the Germans would not stop them, would in fact encourage them. This was done, of course, by individuals with the basest instincts. The Polish workers in our town tried to stop them. The priest Lozowski put up strong resistance, called upon the people to oppose such criminal behavior, but the intoxication of looting was irresistible.)

Several days pass this way. The Jews themselves are now waiting impatiently for the Germans, for they will certainly put a stop to such violence. Although the approach of the German army is frightening, the present situation is worse. People cannot live this way for long. Our vulnerability is obvious, but we can do nothing.

The next few days brought news of the disintegration of the Soviet Army in Poland and of the rapid advances of the German Army. We began to hear stories that, as the Germans occupied cities and towns, they brought in special forces, the SS and Gestapo, who burned Jewish homes, killed Jews indiscriminately, and terrorized the survivors.

Within days we could see that the Soviet Army, or what was left of it, was withdrawing, and we knew that the Germans were near. On Saturday night and early Sunday morning, the German army came into town, and the burning and killing began.

Feitche's words:

Soon the military is fully awake. First they carry out of the synagogue the Torah scrolls that Jews have not managed to hide. With their helpers from the town they pour gasoline over the scrolls and set fire to them. Laughing in glee, they stand around watching the Torah scrolls burn.

Finished with the synagogue, they turn their attention to the Jewish homes, break open doors, invite the Poles to take whatever they please. But the most valuable things the Germans take for themselves. Their helpers grab whatever is left. A joyous time is beginning for them. And why not? They can see that the Germans are right—Jews have all the wealth, which they will now "inherit" quickly and easily. Their only regret is that they cannot take everything their eyes see; they can't decide what to take first. Peasants who live closer to Jasionowka drive their wagons into town. Those who live farther store the stolen goods in places close to town and go back for more. It's too good an opportunity to let pass. They can pile up enough things now to last a lifetime.

SS men, accompanied by Polish collaborators, went through town using flame throwers to burn Jewish homes and shoot people trying to escape the fires. Loudspeakers announced that all Jews must go to the square and line up against the church wall.

As for our family, since we lived about two miles from the center of town, we decided to run and hide in the woods several miles from our home. There, in the woods, we spent the night. In the morning a group of young Polish men came searching for us on their way to church. They found us, assaulted us, and beat us without mercy. One young man found an old fence post and with it hit my father until my father was covered with blood and blind in one eye. They dragged him to a nearby creek, threw him in, and drove the rest of us towards town, telling us that the Germans were lining the Jews up against the church wall to be executed. When we reached the town, we were informed that the shooting of the Jews at the church wall had not taken place.

Those who were at the church wall later told us that after they had stood there for several hours facing machine guns, a high-ranking officer had driven up and made a speech. He told them that to shoot them now would let them off too easily; that eventually they would be killed; that before that happened, they would be expected to work, to suffer, and to give up all of their possessions. They would be killed when the Germans were good and ready. With such promises for the future, the exhausted 1500 or so Jews were dismissed. All this time our Polish neighbors had stood there cheering the Germans on. A few even had asked the Germans for permission to do some of the shooting so they might share in the joy. The Germans disappointed them.

Most Jews no longer had homes to go back to. During the first twenty-four hours since coming into town, the Germans and Polish collaborators had destroyed most of the Jewish homes and had killed approximately 150 people.

Upon being allowed to go home, several members of our family ran back to the woods where we found our father still alive and brought him home. He asked us to let him die, but we were determined to nurse him back to life.

We took in several other families whose houses had been destroyed and allowed them to share our home. Thus, there were over twenty people crowding our small house now. In the house next to ours, several families from town moved in with our neighbors. Amongst the new families was a shoemaker who took me in as an apprentice. Thus, at thirteen, I learned to fix and make new shoes.

My apprenticeship was short, and I never learned all a shoemaker needs to know. I do remember making a pair of shoes for a customer only to find that I used a *kopite* (form) for the right foot that was several sizes larger than the form I used for the left foot. No wonder I remain a *Schuster* (shoemaker) in name only!

Between June, 1941, and January 25, 1943, when the entire town was "liquidated," life in Jasionowka was pure hell. We suffered as much or more at the hands of our Polish neighbors than we did at the hands of the Germans. The situation resembled an ongoing pogrom that never ended. The Germans ordered the Jews to appoint a *Judenrat* (a group of prominent Jews to whom the Germans could deliver demands). Demands for money, gold, goods, and so forth were made almost daily. If a demand was not met, the Germans thought nothing of rounding up a number of Jews and executing them. Often, the Germans would come into town, round up a number of young men to do a certain job, such as snow cleaning, and execute them at the end of the assignment.

Feitche writes about this:

> *It happened that at that time the Germans ordered the establishment of a Jewish "leadership body" that could act for the town's Jews — the so-called* Judenrat, *or Jewish Council. No one volunteers for that service, however, and thus the committee of seven has no choice but to become the* Judenrat *of Jasionowka.*
>
> *At that time our town did not yet have its own kommisar; we were subject to the authority of the Knyszyn kommissariat. One day the Germans order all Jews to come out into the street for a roll-call. No one knows where they will be taken or when they will be brought back. The* Judenrat *tries to find out what the Germans want of us. Perhaps it is a trap. When the* Judenrat *learns that it is only a roll-call to select able-bodied men for work, they ask everyone to report. They themselves are first in line. Jews put on clean clothes and come out into the street.*
>
> *Everyone wants to work. It is known that Jews who do not have jobs will be deported. Many of the town's factories had been burned down. There are not enough jobs for everyone in the town. Many of the younger men have gone off to find work in the villages as farm-hands, the older Jews as shepherds. Still, almost half remain unemployed. The* Judenrat *acts energetically on this and people begin to earn a little money. By various means they succeed in keeping everyone safe, for the time being.*

We had little to hope for. The news that reached us during that period of 1941-1942 was all bad. The Germans were at the gates of Moscow, Leningrad in the north, and Stalingrad in the south. Most of Europe was either German-occupied or under German influence. Worst of all, rumors began to reach us of entire communities being liquidated and taken to concentration camps, where all kinds of killing took place, including gassing in gas chambers. As Jewish communities were being liquidated in cities and towns, a few individuals would escape. Some came to Jasionowka and told stories which were almost incomprehensible and unbelievable. What were we to do?

My father, though blinded in one eye and quite weak, had survived the assault upon him during the first day of German occupation. He urged the family to take whatever steps could be taken to prepare for the expected liquidation of our town. First he and the other adult members of our

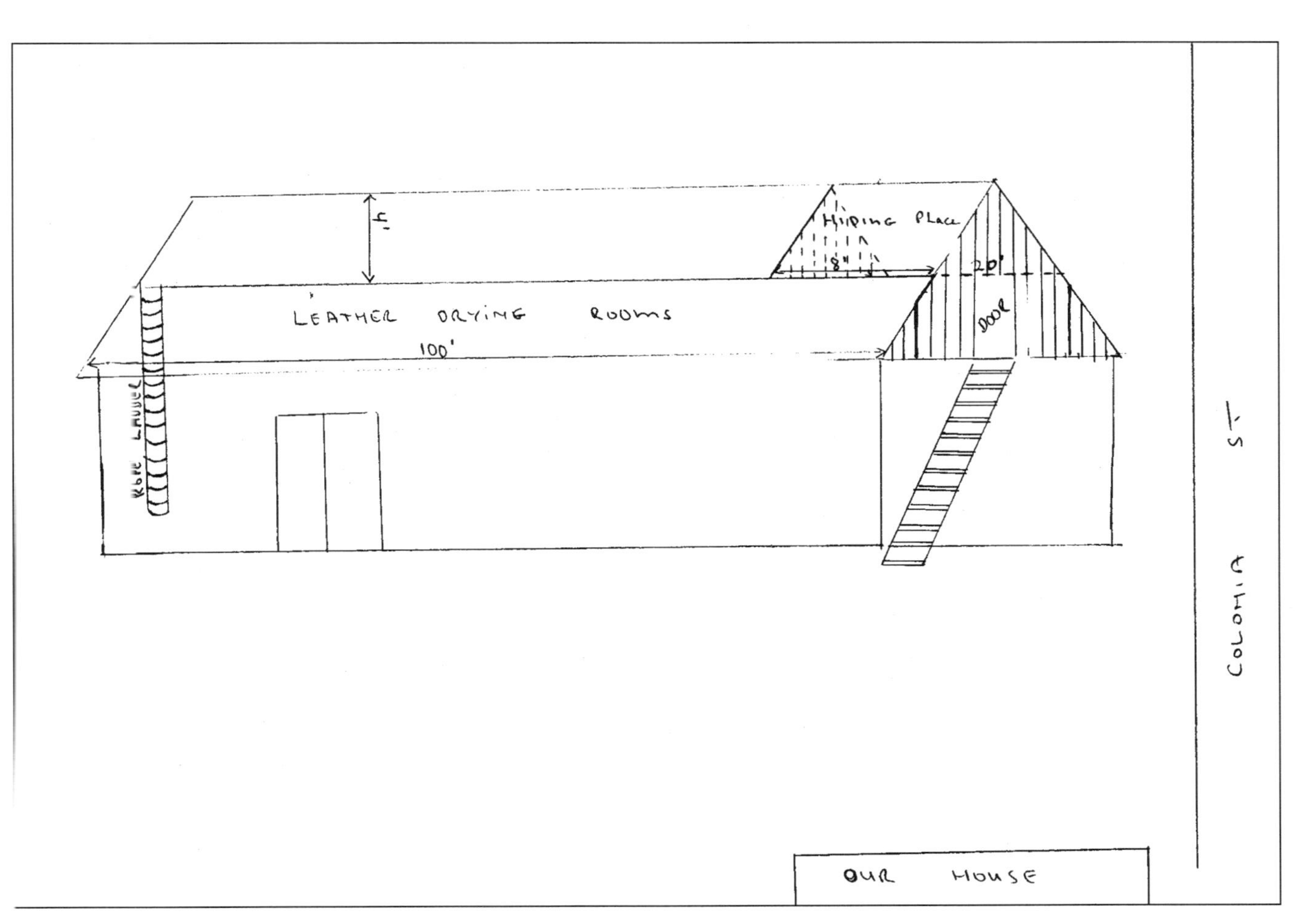

Our hiding place over the tannery.

family decided that we needed places where we could hide during each roundup of young Jews. It was also decided that we needed a place where a larger number could hide when the inevitable final liquidation came.

For a quick hiding place, we created a small space over a porch which could be reached from the attic of our house. There, my older brothers and brothers-in-law would run each time a raid was conducted for a "special job" from which no one ever returned.

As for a more substantial hiding place, it was created above the tannery and was quite ingenious. It could hold as many as fifteen or sixteen people. Above is a sketch of what it was like. By climbing up a rope ladder at the far end of the tannery you reached a crawl space about 3 1/2 to 4 feet high and about twenty-feet wide. In total darkness, on your hands and knees, you crawled to the front end of the crawl space about eighty or ninety feet, and there you could slide open the trap door. Once in the hiding place, you could put the trap door into place and lock it. Anyone looking for us, if they were to come into the crawl space, would find nothing but a blank wall.

They would never know that beyond that wall, the crawl space continued and that people were hiding there.

In addition to the hiding places, my family found a farmer who lived near a forest who agreed to give us shelter and hide us from the Germans if we would give him money, gold, leather, and practically everything we owned.

LIQUIDATION OF JASIONOWKA

You, my dearest grandchildren, will want to know what happened to me during the period of German occupation and beyond. Although my recollections are fading, and my memory is diminished, I will do my best to tell you all that I still do remember.

During the nights of January 24 and 25, 1943, Jasionowka was surrounded by about 300 Gestapo troops. They drove their trucks through the streets and announced over loudspeakers that all Jews must report to the center of town immediately to be transported and resettled. Anyone who failed to do so would be executed on the spot. The Polish police and our neighbors were happy to help the Germans carry out the roundup. See the map entitled "Deportation, Massacre and Revolt, January 1943" on the next page.

Those of our family who could, ran to the hiding place above the tannery. About a dozen adults, not family members, who had been living in our house, also joined us. We did not have time to dress and took whatever blankets and quilts we could find for cover. We said quick good-byes to those of our family and others who lived in our house but could not hide. They had small children who might cry out and give us away. Quick good-byes to brothers, sisters, nieces, and nephews we loved and would never see again.

Cracks in the walls of our hiding place allowed us to see what was going on in the street below us. We saw Jews being driven towards town, heard the cries and the fatal shots.

Bolek Bortnik and his family, our neighbors from across the street, were frantic. They did not see us marching off to the center of town and desperately wanted us dead so that they could occupy our house. They knew that we were hiding someplace, and they constantly brought Germans to our property hoping to find us. In our tannery there was a large steam boiler, and Bolek fired his rifle through the boiler to see if we were hiding inside.

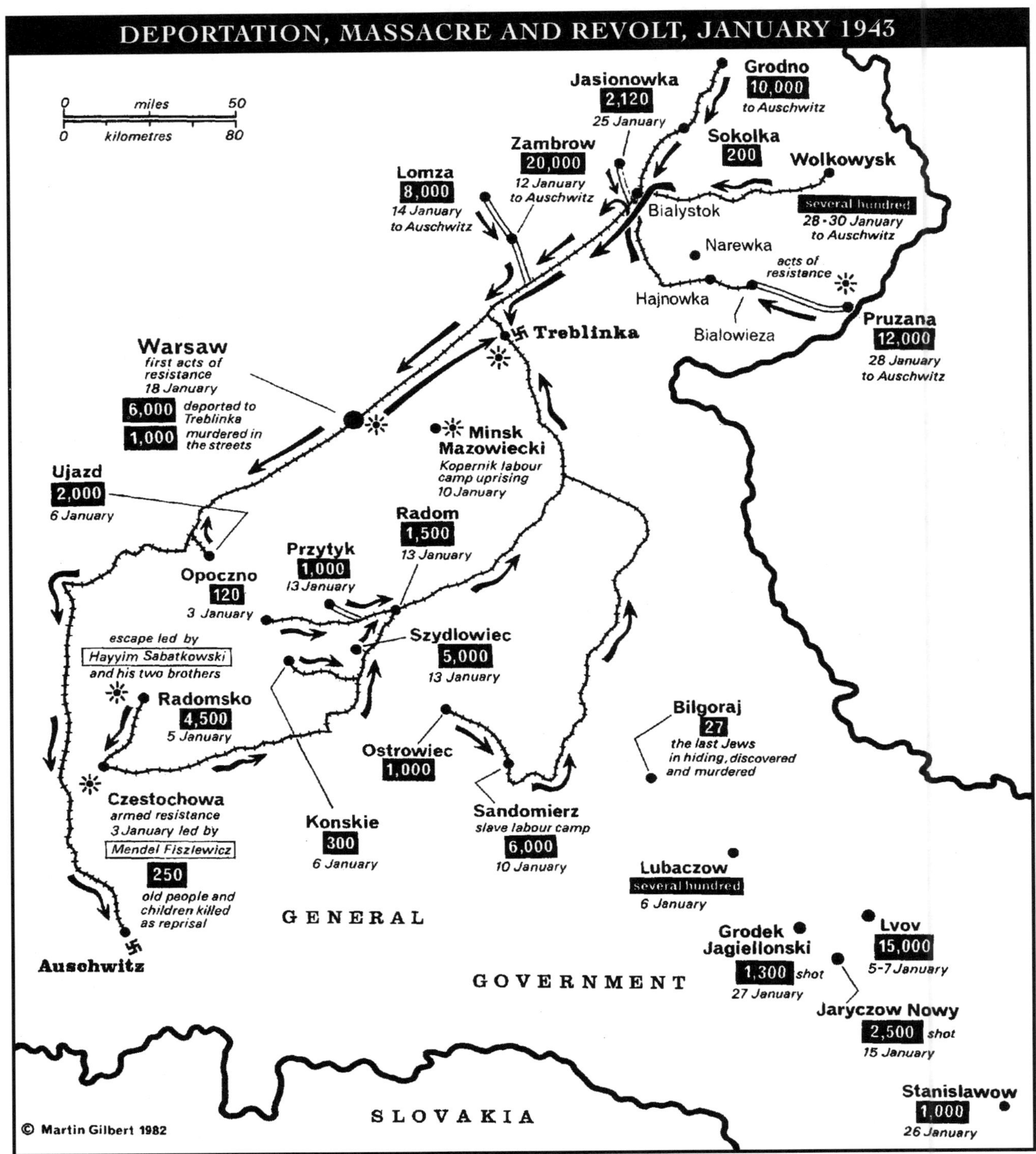

From THE MACMILLAN ATLAS OF THE HOLOCAUST by Martin Gilbert. Pg. 142

After most of the Jews were taken away from Jasionowka, an eerie silence fell upon the town. Now and then the silence was broken by shots fired at Jews who had been hiding and were trying to flee town under cover of darkness.

We stayed in the hiding place for two days and two nights, without food or clothing, but could stay there no longer. We decided to make a run for it, two at a time, until we reached the woods where we planned to meet up and go to the farmer who had promised to give us shelter. My father, who was not well, and I, at age 14 the youngest of the children, would be the first to attempt the escape. Covered with white sheets for camouflage, my father and I crawled on our hands and knees as far as we could and ran until we reached the woods. My mother and youngest sister, Tzipe, were not so lucky. The Germans, still watching the fields around Jasionowka, spotted them, and opened fire. We never saw them again.

My father and I reached the farmer. Despite the fact that we had paid his price, he refused to let us in or give us warm clothes or food. In fact, he ordered us to leave, threatening to call the Germans if we did not. Half-frozen and starving, we went back to the woods where my father soon died. Alone, with no place to go, I decided to go back to town and give up the fight to stay alive. As I headed towards town a Polish farm woman, the wife of Wladislaw Czarniecki (I don't recall her first name), stopped me and asked me where I was going. She offered to give me shelter in a barn, which contained pigs on the ground level and straw and hay above. There she brought me food and medicine whenever she could and made me promise that each day I would say, "I will die tomorrow, but not today."

Not today. Not today. Why not? Alone, except for the pigs below, and rats and mice everywhere, I dug into the hay loft, waiting for I knew not what. Would the war ever end? Would the German murderers ever be defeated? Would I be the only Jew left alive? Could life ever be worth living again? Without any hope, I waited. Days and weeks I waited, until one night two young men from Jasionowka, Ruven (Ruvak) Goniondzky and his brother, Chone, came to beg for food. Mrs. Czarniecki told them that I was hiding in the barn, and she brought them to me. They invited me to join them in their journey, and I did.

Thus, for the next eighteen months, until we were liberated, my destiny was tied to the destiny of Ruvak, Chone, and a third young man from Jasionowka, Shimon Zlatarinski. The four of us struggled to survive by hiding in the forest. At times we hid with a poor farmer, Dekar, who lived in a forest near the village of Stoke. The Dekars were willing to let us dig an underground bunker in a shed where they kept pigs. There we spent days underground and nights above ground hiding in the hay and straw. Some nights we would risk our lives to beg for food, mostly bread and salted bacon.

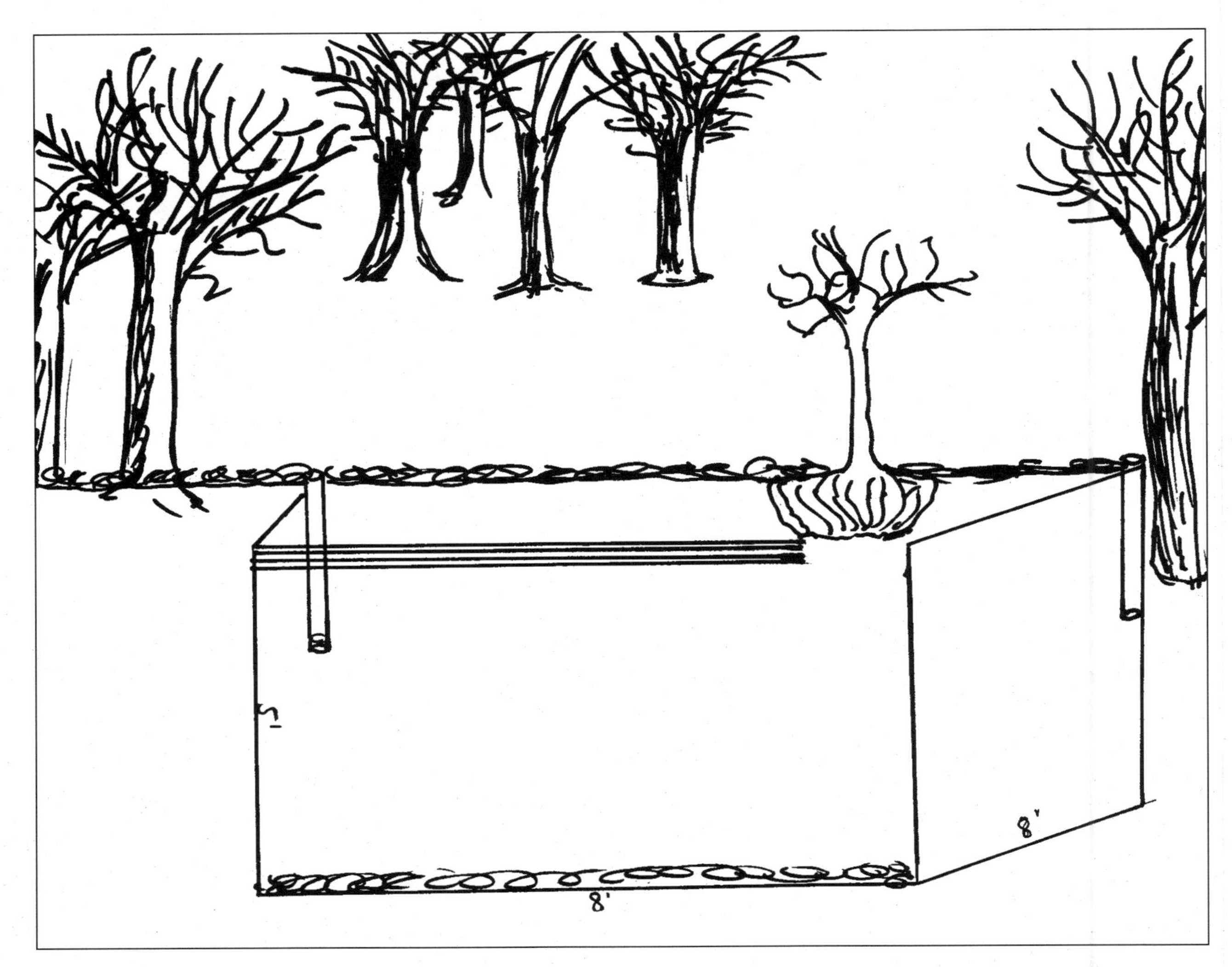

Our underground bunker.

A good part of the time we spent hiding in the forest. There we built an underground bunker which was quite ingenious.

We found an area overgrown with trees and shrubs where farmers were not likely to bring their cattle to graze. With not more than an ax or two, a couple of shovels, and several burlap bags, we would select a spot free of large trees and roots where a young light tree could be converted to an entrance door. The earth we dug out had to be carried, sack by sack, far away and disbursed in such a way as to be unnoticed. Also, the young trees we chopped down for support beams had to be brought from far away, one by one, in order to leave no trace of activity near our bunker. We lined the floor of the bunker with soft branches to serve as our bed. We provided ventilation through short pipes which protruded just above the earth cover, where loose leaves concealed the ends of the pipes from view. We lived like animals in the forest, except that animals have the natural ability to hunt as they please and roam freely. We were constantly hunted, had little food, and were unable to obtain food without risking our lives. Worst of all, we had no way to clean ourselves.

One summer night, when the wheat was high and almost ready to be harvested, Ruvak and I went out to beg for food in a village about five miles away. As we left the village to return to our hiding place, the full moon had come out, and it was quite bright. We were on a narrow path with wheat growing on each side when suddenly, from nowhere, several young Polish men with guns appeared. The minute they realized we were Jews in hiding, they started shooting. I saw Ruvak fall in the wheat field on one side of the path just as I went down in the wheat on the other side of the path. I crawled on my hands and knees for a while, and after a while I whistled our secret tune but got no response from Ruvak. I assumed that he was dead and ran as fast as I could to the forest bunker to tell the others what had happened. About one-half hour later Ruvak came running, and as he approached he shouted that I had been killed. It was a happy reunion that I will never forget.

By 1944, the Polish farmers had heard rumors that the Germans were being pushed back from Russia and were likely to lose the war. This encouraged them to help the Jews in hiding by giving them some food and information. The news certainly helped our spirits and made us more determined than ever to go on enduring our difficulties in order to outlive Hitler.

I can't recall the exact date when we discovered that we were liberated. Most likely it was November or December of 1944. As we returned to the outskirts of Jasionowka, we discovered that several members of my family had also survived. I was reunited with my oldest sister Baile and her daughter Roske; my next older sister Feitche; my brother Maishe; and my cousins Shleime, Elie Chaim, and Maishe Shuster. We also discovered that a total of 82 people, out of approximately 2000 Jews of Jasionowka, had survived. My cousin, Shleime, as head of the Jasionowka committee, compiled a list of survivors and their whereabouts as of 1946, a copy of which can be found on the next two pages. It is written in Yiddish. As can be seen from the list, by March of 1946 not a single Jew remained in Jasionowka. The list gives the name of each survivor, his or her parents' names, and his or her place of residence in 1946.

I don't know the details regarding the fate of other members of my family who did not survive. From my cousins and others who were rounded up and shipped off to a concentration camp know as Treblinka, see map on page 32, I learned that my brother Maier was killed when he jumped from their fast-moving train. The freight car in which my brother, his wife Rena, and their baby were riding was packed with some 150 people, including my Uncle Mordche Schuster and his children Shleime, Elie Chaim, and Maishe, and their families. My uncle urged the young people to tear out an opening where the small window was at the top of the car and to jump.

1945 גאמבין

פון [illegible] 1937

ליסטע

פון לעבן געבליבענע יאשינאווקער יידן.

נ.ז.	פאמיליע און נאמען	נעמען פון עלטערן	דער איצטיקער אדרעס
1	שוסטער שלומה	מרדכי איטקע	ביאליסטאק
2	" אליהו חיים	" "	"
3	" משה	" "	"
4	" פיישטע	יענקל חיה-שרה	"
5	שוסטער-קלאטניצקאביילע	" " "	"
6	קלאטניצקא ראזא	לייבוש ביילע	"
7	האלפערן שלמה	פסח הענניע	"
8	" אברהם	" "	"
9	פערמאן אברהם-מרדכי	משה	"
10	" ציווליע	"	"
11	פערמאן-באלגליי דאבע	"	"
12	באלגליי רישע	דאבע	"
13	טוראסקי יצחק	אברהם לייב שרה	"
14	" מאשע	" " "	"
15	" יאסל	יצחק פייגל	"
16	פאפלאווסקי שלום	טאניע חיה	"
17	" רחל	" "	"
18	" לייב	" "	"
19	קאניע קלמן לייב	וועלוול חיה עבדל	"
20	זלאטארינסקי שמעון	דוד ברײנקע	"
21	גאלדמאן גרשון	מלכה	"
22	ראזענבלום חנה	אברהם פרומע	"
23	סידראנסקי יצחק	זיידקע שאשקע	"
24	" אברהם	" "	"
25	שוסטער משה	יענקל חיה שרה	איטאליען
26	" בערל	" " "	"
27	האלפערן בנימין	[illegible]	"
28	האלפערן ישראל	" "	רוסלאנד
29	פרידמאן אלטער	ישראל יענקל	איטאליען
30	" אברהם	אלטער פרומע	"
31	קרינסקי שמואל	אהרן גוטקע	"
32	" מיכל	" "	"
33	" גוטקע	שמואל מיכל	"
34	קאמינסקי לייב	מאטל הענניע	"
35	" באצקל	שלמה מיטע	
36	" יוסף	סענדער שרה שאשע	פויליש מיליטער
37	רובינשטיין אהרן	שלמה שרה	"
38	פאפלאווסקי ראובן	אפרים שיינע	איטאליען
39	" אברהם	זכריה מיטע	"
40	" דוד	" "	"
41	גאניאנדזקי ראובן	מאטל לייקע	ארץ-ישראל
42	" חנאן	" "	"
43	" ישראל	אברהם רייזל	לאדזש
44	" משה	" "	ארץ-ישראל
45	" פייוול	ברוך חיה-סלאווע	סאוויעטן-פארבאנד
46	בערנארד יהושע	משה עלקע	ארץ-ישראל
47	ראדזי חנה	דוד מירעשע	איטאליען
48	[illegible] מאיר	אברהם שרה-רחל	ארץ-ישראל
49	לעוואר זיידקע	לייבל רבקה	" "
50	" פסח	בערל מלכה	איטאליען
51	ראזענבלאט משה	חיים-לייזער חוה-גיטל	ארץ-ישראל
52	וואשליקאווסקי שמואל	שמחה ראשקע	" "
53	הוסמאן-ראדזי אסתר-צירל	מערקע	" "
54	וואשליקאווסקי מאיר	דוד חנה	
55	" משה	" "	" "
56	דובסקי יענקל	אברהם-יצחק טימע	איטאליען
57	פערמאן יענקל	הערש באבל	ארץ-ישראל
58	גרין יאסל	אברהם	סאוויעט-רוסלאנד
59	יאנאווסקי שמואל	יענקל באשקע	" "
60	פערלשטיין חיים (פון וואשליקאווע)	יצחק	" "

List of Jewish Survivors (1946)

ליסטע

ון ~~[illegible]~~ לעבן געבליבענע יאשינאווקער ידן.

ל.נ.	פאמיליע און נאמען	נעמען פון עלטערן	דער איצטיקער אדרעס
61.	סוראסקי זלמן	מרדכי שאשקע	סאוויעט-רוסלאנד
62.	אסטראבורסקי באשקע	שימע קיילע	" "
63.	" רחל	" "	" "
64.	ראזענבערג חיה	אפרים מלכה-רייזל	
65.	ביילאך שלום	ישראל פע[illegible]יקע	" "
66.	קאמיאנסקי באשע	מאטל העניע	" "
67.	" משה	" "	" "
68.	מארגנבערג קלמן	הערשל שרה	איטאליען
69.	פינקעלשטיין שעפסל	לייבוש פראדל	ארץ-ישראל
70.	אזריקאן פינקעלשטיין ליבע	מאיר דבורה	" "
71.	לאכמאן יענקל	מאטיע(דער שטעפער)	איטאליען
72.	" יוסף	יענקל מינטשע	"
73.	גלוגאווסקי לייזער	אברהם יצחק פיכלע	איטאליען
74.	" העניע	" " "	"
75.	מינסקי חיים	יהושע פייגל מערקע	סאוויעטן-פארבאנד
76.	" גושע	" " "	" "
77.	" שפרה	" " "	" "
78.	" טייבע	" " "	" "
79.	" יודל	" " "	" "
80.	" ביילע	" " "	" "
81.	" מאניעק	משה אידע	" "
82.	" סעמעק	" "	
[illegible]			

פארזיצער פון יאשינאווקער קאמיטעט

ש. [illegible]

Żydowskiej ... w Jasionówce

ביאליסטאק 15.3 46

Most able-bodied young people did jump. Shleime, Elie Chaim, Maishe and others survived. Others were killed by the German guards or by the train itself. Many who did escape were caught by Poles or Germans and killed. Some died and were thrown in shallow graves in nearby fields or forests.

The reunions were bittersweet. We quickly realized that our Polish neighbors had desperately hoped that none of us would survive and were terribly disappointed to see some of us alive. They had taken over our houses and were not about to give back our property. Chaos prevailed. The war was still going on, and there were no authorities willing or able to help us.

My sisters, my brother and I decided to live in the house owned by my cousin Shleime, a large house at the end of Colonia Street about a mile further away from the center of town than our own house. We spent the days and nights talking about our fate and sharing our experiences of the last several years, and trying to make some sense out of all that had happened. What were we to do now?

We soon learned that the Polish anti-Semites had formed an organization called *Akcia Krayeva* (A-K) dedicated to completing the job Hitler had failed to execute fully. They went from town to town attacking and killing off the few Jews who had managed to survive. Since very few Jews had survived, the job of finishing them off was not difficult.

Jasionowka was an exception. With close to 100 Jews surviving, the A-K planned to start the final slaughter by wiping out our family where they suspected they would find the most resistance.

We now lived in a wooden house with windows, wooden shutters, a basement, and a staircase to the attic. In the house with me were my cousin Shleime; his friend Yankl Dunsky, who had lost both his legs as a result of frost; my brother, Maishe; my sisters, Baile and Feitche; my niece Roske; and several other women who were staying with us. Each afternoon before dark, we would close the shutters, lock the doors, and spend the evening talking, drinking tea, and trembling in fear whenever someone approached the house. In addition to taking these precautions, we had obtained several rifles, pistols, hand grenades, and other ammunition. Whoever went to answer a knock at the door would do so with a pistol in hand.

One Thursday afternoon at the end of March, 1945, my cousin Elie Chaim had gone out to see a neighbor. Baile was baking *challah* and other delicacies for the *Shabbat* and the kitchen was full of baking sheets on which braided *challahs* were set out to rise. Just before darkness fell, there was a knock at the door. Maishe, pistol in hand, went to see who was there. When he asked who it was, the reply, in Polish, came: "Open the door. We are friends." He immediately realized that the "friends" were the A-K. Maishe quickly signaled to us and we went into action. We opened the trap door to the basement and ordered the women and children to go downstairs. Only my brother, Maishe, our friend Yankl Dunsky, and I remained on the main floor.

Just then, the AK opened fire from machine guns they had set up all around our house. I still can see the baking sheets and *challahs* flying through the kitchen as the bullets hit them.

After what seemed like hours, the machine guns fell silent. At that point, my brother Maishe and I opened fire to tell our attackers that we were still alive. Yankl Dunsky, without legs, crawled along the floor supplying us with bullets and other ammunition.

At one point we heard someone giving an order to approach and set the house on fire. My brother and I crawled up the stairs to the attic. As several A-K members came close to the house, we threw out a couple of hand grenades. The Poles suffered casualties, including at least one dead, and decided to retreat. This night would end with no further confrontation.

We telephoned our cousin Maishe Shuster in Bialystok where he was an official working for the Soviet police. Several hours later he arrived with a number of trucks, and that day all the Jews of Jasionowka were transported to Bialystok where they could find some safety. This was the last time I saw Jasionowka, the town where I was born and grew up, where I had been nurtured and loved by a large and caring family—a town which remains in my memory not as a dream but as a horrible nightmare, a nightmare from which I have not yet fully recovered.

MY NEW LIFE BEGINS

Having been driven out of Jasionowka again, this time by the Polish A-K, we realized that we could no longer consider Poland our home. The family decided that my brother Maishe, age 21, and I, age 17, look for a way to get to Palestine. We were to find the way, and the rest of the family would follow. By foot, truck, train, wagon or whatever, we pushed across borders, crossing Czechoslovakia, Hungary, Austria, Germany, heading toward Italy.

This movement of survivors across Europe was led by young members of the Haganah, which became the Israeli special forces, who were determined to bring as many survivors as possible to Palestine despite the British policy of keeping Jews out. Britain, who ruled over Palestine pursuant to a League of Nations mandate after World War I, was openly pro-Arab and did all it could to keep Jews out. When, in 1948, the United Nations ordered Britain to give up its mandate and partitioned Palestine, Britain did all it could to help the Arabs take over most of the land and drive out the Jews.

Once we reached southern Italy, we were put into a displaced persons camp for refugees operated by the United Nations Refugee Relief Association. The camp was set up in Santa Cesarea, a coastal town located at the "heel" of the boot-shaped peninsula.

While in the camp, I was approached by Israelis and asked if I would be interested in going back to Poland to bring others out. I agreed to do so. Again, on foot or whichever way possible, I crossed many borders illegally and headed back towards Poland. I gathered up a group, including survivors from Jasionowka, and we started moving throughout Europe towards Italy.

This time we entered Germany by train where I met my dear friend, Sholom Bailach, whose two older brothers had married two of my sisters. I loved Sholom whom I used to see often before Germany attacked the Soviet Union in June of 1941. Sholom was a pilot in the Soviet Air Force

Sholem Bailey (Bailach), his wife Sally, their daughter Paula, my sister Feitche, and my brother-in-law (and cousin) Shleime Schuster at our wedding in 1955.

during the war. When the war was coming to an end in 1945, he was stationed in Germany. There he met a beautiful young blonde woman, Sally, who had been known as Irka during German occupation, hiding her identity and passing as a Polish child. They fell in love and had just married when I ran into Sholom.

He insisted that I let the train go on without me and spend a few days with them after which he would help me catch up with the train and the group I was leading. The train left without me and soon collided with another train. A number of the people in my group were injured, and one man was killed. Once again, I was saved from injury or death. As for Sholom, he and Sally settled in Montreal, Canada, and we have remained close and much more than friends even to this day.

Before we reached Italy again, I was shot by border guards and ended up in an Italian hospital. I still retain a discharge slip showing that I was admitted to the hospital in diLeuca, a neighboring coastal town, on November 27, 1946 and discharged on December 16, 1946. While I was in the hospital, I heard that my mother's sister, Mary Kaufman, who lived in Rochester, New York, had discovered that I had survived and had sent me a ticket to come to the United States.

In Santa Cesarea I was very actively involved with organizations and various causes all related to our struggle to get to

ארגון הפליטים באיטליה
המחלקה לתרבות

הסמינריון למורים
בסנטה מריה די לאוקה

תעודה

התלמיד ....
שנולד .... בעיר ....
גמר את חוק הלמודים בסמינריון
....
ונמצא מוכשר לשמש מורה ומדריך לנוער.
התאריך: ....

יו"ר מרכז ארגון הפליטים

מנהל מחלקת התרבות ומנהל הסמינריון

My teaching diploma.

172/S

Surname - *Cognome* SCHUSTER

Christian Name - *Nome* BERNARD

Nationality - *Nazionalità* POLISH   Sex - *Sesso* M

has permission to be absent from No. 1 Transit Camp (Refugees) between the hours of 0 00 and 22 00 hrs for the purpose of proceeding to and from the town of Bari.

è autorizzato ad assentarsi dal Campo Transito Profughi No. 1 dalle ore 0,00 alle 22,00 per recarsi a Bari e ritonare in Campo.

Unit Stamp.   Signed - *Firmato*

CAMP DIRECTOR

No. 1 Transit Camp (Refugees) - Bari

REFUGEE HOSPITAL DI LEUCA

This is to certify that Schuster Berl

of S. Cesarea

arrived in the Hosital on the 27.XI.46

has been discharged to day the 16.XII.46

to S. Cesarea

S.M.O. Leuca Hospital

Below: Dinner with displaced persons in Italy. Berl is standing in the back row, fourth from the left.

ALLIED EXPEDITIONARY FORCE

D. P. INDEX CARD

1 3030062

1. (Registration number)

SCHUSTER BERNARD

2. (Family name) (Other given names)

3. (Signature of holder)

Above and on next page: Various official papers that Berl kept from his time in Italy.

Palestine. I also enrolled in a seminar for Hebrew teachers organized by Jews from Palestine. I earned a diploma to teach Hebrew and help prepare individuals for eventual life in Palestine (Israel). My diploma is shown on the previous page. I have also included documents and various photos taken in Santa Cesarea, on this and the next few pages, which reflect the hectic life that I and others led there.

I greatly enjoyed life in Santa Cesarea even though it was a displaced persons camp and we were refugees and had no permanent status. My sister Baile and her daughter Roske joined us. The fact that Britain was pro-Arab and tried to keep Jews out of Palestine hurt much, but we were determined and had hopes of reaching Palestine somehow.

N. 36/313

Mod. B

Soggiorno degli Stranieri in Italia

Séjour des Entrangers en Italie - Foreigners' sojourn in Italy - Aufenhaltserkärung für Ausländer in Italien.
(Circolare Ministero Interno N. 443/49566 del 19 gennaio 1947)

Provincia di Bari
Province - Province - Provinz

Comune di Bari
Commune - Municipality - Gemeinde

Cognome Schuster
Nom - Name - Zuname

nome Bernard
prénom - surnam - vername

paternità Jakob
paternité - paternity - Vater

maternità Marecka Sara
maternité - maternity - mutter

nato a Bialystok (Polonia)
né (née) à - place of birth - geboren in

il 17. V. 1927
le - date of birth - am.

di nazionalità polacca
de nationalité - nationality - staatsangehörigkeit

di condizione celibe
de condition - condition - zivilstand

luogo di provenienza Austria
lieu de provenance - coming-from ! - herkunftsort

data di ingresso in Italia giugno 1945
date d'entrée en Italie - date of entrance in Italy - Einresedatum in Italien

scopo del soggiorno profugo ex-internato
but du séjour - reasons of sojourn - zwek d. aufenthaltes

luogo di dimora in Italia Campo Transit 1 Bari
lieu de demeure en Italie - place of dwelling in Italy - aufenthaltsort in Italien

con i congiunti di età non superiore ai 16 anni, a tergo indicati, che accompagnano il dichiarante.
avec des enfants, indiqués au verso, d'âge non superieur à 16 ans, qui accompagnent le déclarant.
with children, whose age does not surpass 16 years of age, listed on the back of this form as living with the declarer.
mit auf der rückseite angeführten, nicht über 16 jahre alten angehörigen, die den erklärer begleiten.

La presente ricevuta deve essere esibita ad ogni richiesta degli organi di Polizia.
Le présent reçu doit être exhibé sur toute demande des officiers ou agents de Police.
This receipt must be shown on request to officials of the Police.
Diese bescheinigung muss auf verlangen den beamten der Polizeibehörde vorgezeigt werden.

Il possesso di essa costituisce la sola prova della dichiarazione di soggiorno.
La possession de ce reçu constitue la seule preuve de la declaration de séjour.
The possession of said receipt is the only proof of the present declaration.
The besitz bildet, nur, den bexeis der anmeldung.

Bari, li 10. III 1947
le - date - den

Firma e qualifica dell'Autorità di P. S.
Signature et qualification de l'Autorité de Sûreté Publique
Signature et qualification of the Police Authority
Unterschrift der Polizeibehörde

PARTE DA CONSEGNARSI AL DICHIARANTE

ANNOTAZIONI

AVVERTENZA — Il titolare è vivamente pregato di restituire il presente documento, all'atto dell'uscita dall'Italia consegnandolo al funzionario addetto alla verifica dei passaporti alla frontiera. Tale restituzione è richiesta unicamente a scopi statistici.
AVERTISSEMENT — Le titulaire est vivement prié, au moment de quitter l'Italie, de consigner le présent document au fonctionnaire qui vérifie les passeports à la frontière. Cette restitution est uniquement demandée dans un but de statistique.
NOTICE — The possessor is requested to return this document to the passport official at the frontier, on leaving Italy. Such restitution is requested only for statistical reasons.
BENACHRICHTIGUNG — Der inhaber wird dringend gebeten, diese dokument beim ueberschreiten der italianischen grenze dem pasabeamten auszahändigen. Diese rueckgabe hat lediglich statistiche zwecke.

(3105063) Roma, 1947 - Istituto Poligrafico dello Stato - G. C.

Berl, his niece Roske, sister Baile and brother Maishe

Berl carrying flag — march to demand right to go to Palestine

Berl all dressed up and posing in front of Displaced Persons camp, where he lived.

Berl studying

Berl in hospital while recuperating from gunshot wounds — brother Maishe in center at top

Taken the day Roske and Baile left for England. Top row: Maishe and Roske are third and fourth from left, Berl, seventh from left. Baile, bottom right.

Berl studying at seminar for Hebrew teachers.

Berl at another demonstration with Palestine Rabbi official.

Berl and his brother Maishe.

Berl and other camp leaders planning a demonstration.

Berl leading a demonstration against the British.

Berl and friends.

Because of the United States immigration laws, designed to keep most refugees from eastern Europe out, neither my brother nor my sisters were able to go to the United States. I was still a minor, and thanks to a special law allowing selected minors to enter the United States, I was able to obtain a visa.

My family and I talked it over and decided that I should go to the United States and eventually move to Palestine or try to bring some of my family members to the United States. However, before I was in a position to bring any member of my family to the United States, my sister Baile and her daughter left Italy for England and eventually Australia. My brother Maishe was able to follow them.

On May 12, 1947, I sailed from Naples, Italy, on a small boat, the "Marine Perch." The crossing was difficult. The boat, without stabilizers, tossed in the rough seas so that most people aboard became seasick. A short romance with a lively Italian girl, who was on her way to the United States to marry an American GI, helped pass the ten-day crossing.

While on the boat I also began to learn my first few words of English. Although at the time I could carry on a conversation in six languages, English was totally foreign to me. I learned my

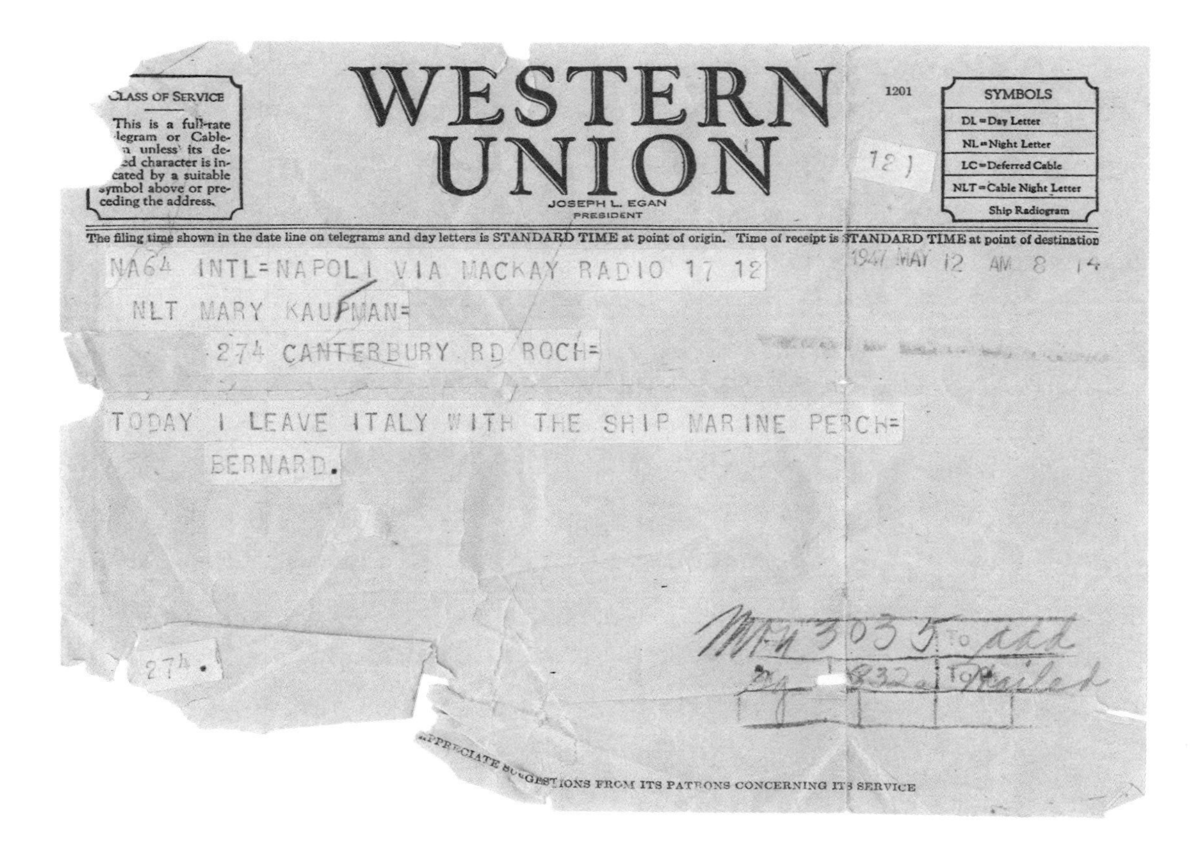
WESTERN UNION

JOSEPH L. EGAN, PRESIDENT

1201

CLASS OF SERVICE: This is a full-rate Telegram or Cablegram unless its deferred character is indicated by a suitable symbol above or preceding the address.

SYMBOLS: DL = Day Letter; NL = Night Letter; LC = Deferred Cable; NLT = Cable Night Letter; Ship Radiogram

The filing time shown in the date line on telegrams and day letters is STANDARD TIME at point of origin. Time of receipt is STANDARD TIME at point of destination

NA64 INTL=NAPOLI VIA MACKAY RADIO 17 12 1947 MAY 12 AM 8 14

NLT MARY KAUFMAN=

274 CANTERBURY RD ROCH=

TODAY I LEAVE ITALY WITH THE SHIP MARINE PERCH=

BERNARD.

274.

APPRECIATE SUGGESTIONS FROM ITS PATRONS CONCERNING ITS SERVICE

My uncle Willie Kaufman, my cousin Bernice, her husband Bernie Wolk and my aunt Mary at our wedding 1955.

first few words of English when the boat's loudspeaker announced meals each day.

I arrived in New York City on May 22, 1947. I was met by Philip and Evelyn (Chashe) Lichtenstein, their son, Berl, and daughter, Judy. The Lichtensteins were distant relatives who had big hearts and greeted all relatives with open arms. Their modest fifth floor apartment in the Bronx, which had no elevator, became known as the Lichtenstein Hotel. There was always room for anyone in the family who needed a place to sleep. The Lichtensteins liked me and quickly decided that they now had two sons, both named Berl.

When I arrived in the United States I had fairly long hair, of which I was very proud. A day or two after I arrived, Philip took me down the street to a neighborhood barber shop. There he told the barber— in English, which I could not understand—to keep me turned away from the mirror and to keep cutting until he, Philip, said enough. When they were finished I looked in the mirror and cried. Most of my beautiful hair was gone! All I had left now of what I had brought from Europe consisted of the clothing I wore, a cardboard suitcase with an extra pair of pants, a shirt or two, some underwear, and $1.59 in American money. I had nothing else, not even the curls I had grown for so many years.

After about ten days in New York City, Berl Lichtenstein traveled with me to Rochester by train where I was to meet my aunt Mary, her husband, Willie, and begin my new life.

Aunt Mary, my mother's sister, was born in Sztabin, a town not far from Jasionowka, where my mother, too, had been born. She came to the United States in the early part of the twentieth century as a young girl of about sixteen. She went to work in a clothing factory and became an expert at sewing button holes in fine men's garments. She saved every cent she could and accumulated what was then considered a fair amount of money. I was told that aunt Mary was befriended by a handsome man who promised to marry her as soon as he became successful in business. He asked aunt Mary to give him the money she had saved up to help him with his business ventures. After she gave him all of her money, he promptly disappeared never to be seen again.

Lovely, but poor, aunt Mary was despondent. She had lost all hope. Just then a matchmaker came to her with an offer. William (Willie) Kaufman, a young man who had never gone to school beyond the fourth grade but was now a successful businessman and owned a slaughter house in Canandaigua, needed a wife and mother for his infant son, Milton. Willie's first wife had died in childbirth. Mary, desperate and depressed, agreed to marry Willie and lived to regret it.

Willie was good-hearted but totally uneducated and ignorant. He had a strange sense of humor. All in all, he was very difficult to take. Fortunately he was away from home most of the time buying sheep by the trainload. He came home only occasionally. Aunt Mary kept their modest house at 274 Canterbury Road as if it were a palace. She was the finest of homemakers, and her cooking and baking surpassed anything I have ever tasted.

I arrived in Rochester when Milton was no longer around. He had taken off for places unknown. Mary and Willie's only child, Bernice, was about to be married to Bernie Wolk.

Aunt Mary loved me as if I were her son and showed concern for me from the day I arrived. She took me to her dentist, who claimed that in all his professional life he had never seen anyone with such neglected teeth. This neglect was the result of years of hunger and lack of hygiene. My aunt also arranged and paid for several English lessons.

After I had been with them for about a month, Mary and Willie wanted to have a talk with me. In Yiddish, my aunt told me how much they liked me and that they felt the time had come for me to join Willie in the slaughterhouse. They assured me that I would quickly learn the business and that some day the business would be mine. I responded by saying that although I appreciated their offer, I could not accept it. I told them I felt a need to learn English and to go to high school, college, and law school so that I might be in a position to help others and perhaps improve the world in some small way.

After hearing me out, my aunt Mary turned to Willie and in English, so that I would not understand, she said, "Poor boy, he lost his mind as a result of the Holocaust. We must take him to a doctor." In Yiddish she told me that what I had suggested was totally unrealistic and out of reach. She said that people who speak English had to attend high school for four years, college for four years, and law school for at least three years. Since I did not speak English, she told me that I would be a grandfather before I achieved my goals. Feeling very sorry for me, she began to cry.

I assured my aunt and uncle that I understood their concerns. I told them I was determined to give it a try and that I would find a room somewhere and get a job, hopefully before school began in September. With the help of a neighbor, Reuben Goldman, a lawyer who spoke Yiddish fluently, I got a job working for Noah's Ark, a business owned by Noah Sher. My job was to load and stack crated bicycles by the thousands, working nine hours a day.

As for a place to live, I was lucky. As I said earlier, I had an uncle, Irving Meyers, in Rochester. He, his wife Minnie, and their two children, Phyllis and Harvey, lived on Tyler Street. Aunt Minnie and her entire family treated me as if I were a long-lost and very deserving child of theirs. Aunt Minnie's parents, Zelda and Victor Weintraub, then in their 80's, lived in a small house at 124 Alphonse Street. They needed someone to help them take care of the house and offered me a room in exchange for my help. They were so concerned for my welfare that when I slept or rested, "Grandma Zelda" would not permit her own grandchildren to come in, telling them that I was working and studying very hard and needed rest and could not be disturbed.

My stay on Alphonse Street was short since the Weintraubs had to give up the house before long. I then found a room with a family, Ann and Leo Mink, on Conkey Avenue where I stayed—again being treated like a member of the family—until I left to live on campus at the University of Rochester.

An entire chapter describing aunt Minnie would be less than she deserves. Minnie, a true *Yiddishe Mame* was just that to me. Minnie could prepare a meal like no other person I have ever known. She made sure I was at her dinner table for Friday night dinners very often. Her *tsimmes*, (carrots, potatoes, prunes, meat and *kneidlach*), always reminded me of my mother and her cooking. Even after Jane and I were married, and for about 40 years thereafter, our freezer was always full of aunt Minnie's *tsimmes*, barley soup, and *mandel broit*. Aunt Minnie died not long ago, and I miss her terribly. Fortunately her daughter Phyllis and son Harvey remain devoted cousins to this day.

I enrolled at East Evening High School on Alexander Street, about a twenty minute walk from the warehouse where I worked. After working all day, I would wash up, stop at a little restaurant on Main Street, now The Penguin, for something to eat, and proceed to school.

Noah Sher took an interest in me. Noah had a son, Martin, who was my age and was already in college hoping to become a politician. Several times a week Noah would call me on the office warehouse speaker and ask me, in Yiddish, where I was. He would order me to take a nap so that I would be rested for school. Every now and then he would call me into the office and hand me $20 or $50 to supplement my meager wages.

At East Evening High School I met Carlos deZafra. Carlos remained my closest friend until his tragic death some 20 years later. Carlos was vice-principal of East Evening High School. From the moment we met, he became like a father to me. Since I had to stay in school quite late each evening, he offered to drive me home after class. He also opened his home to me. He and his wife, Dorothea, treated me like a member of their family.

Carlos listened to my concerns about my late start learning English and getting a high school education. He suggested that we write to the State Education Department in Albany and ask for permission for me to attend three classes an hour. I was given permission to do so, and with Carlos' help, it worked. At the end of one year I had completed all required Regents courses but one, and after taking intermediate algebra during the summer of 1948, I received a high school diploma

Refugee Gets School Diploma in Year

Youth Attends Night Classes; Gets Scholarship to UR

A 21-year-old former displaced person has earned his college-entrance diploma after only a year of formal high school education—all of it in Rochester public schools.

SCHUSTER

The youth is Bernard Schuster of 551 Conkey Ave., who has a European background of family tragedy, wartime service with Polish and Russian armed forces and self-education in a displaced persons camp.

For his "amazing drive toward attaining further education," he has been granted a $250 loan for study at the University of Rochester by the Sisterhood of Temple B'rith Kodesh.

Here 16 Months

Schuster came to Rochester 16 months ago from a refugee camp in Italy. Although he had never been in a high school, the State Education Department gave him regents credit for his knowledge of the Polish and Russian languages.

A year ago this month he entered East Evening High School and, supporting himself by working days in a warehouse, he averaged more than 85 per cent in courses in English (he capsuled four years of work into one), Algebra, American history, world history and physics.

When the evening school classes ended last June, Schuster switched to Monroe Summer High School. There, while going to school in the morning and working in the afternoon, he completed studies in intermediate algebra and German—and earned his high school diploma.

Lost 20 Pounds

"It took a lot of work and concentration—I had to study until after 2 o'clock most mornings and I lost 20 pounds in the last 12 weeks — but it was worth it," Schuster said yesterday.

David Crystal, executive director of the Jewish Social Service Bureau, said Schuster "typifies the American philosophy of pulling himself up by his own bootstraps."

Schuster had a bitter taste of warfare at the age of 14, when Nazi troops invaded his home near Bialystok, Poland. His mother was killed by gunfire and, after their home was destroyed, his father froze to death in his arms. Two of his sisters and two of his brothers were cremated in the concentration camp at Auschwitz.

Praises Evening School

In Rochester he has been aided in his quest for knowledge by the Jewish Education Association and the Jewish Social Service Bureau.

Schuster said he has "a special debt of gratitude" to faculty members as East Evening High School "who gave me help and encouragement whenever I needed it."

The evening school, he added, "offers more opportunity than most people realize; it's as good as any other school."

And, though Schuster will be entering the university this month, he's going back to evening school too—he wants to study typing.

Article celebrating my high school graduation (September 9, 1948).

Kappa Nu Fraternity
ALPHA CHAPTER
University of Rochester
Rochester, New York

CERTIFICATE OF SCHOLARSHIP
to BERNARD SCHUSTER
March 5, 1949

Dear Bernard,

We the active members of Alpha Chapter, Kappa Nu, and we, the members of the Rochester Grad Club of Kappa Nu take great pride in welcoming you into our Brotherhood.

As a mark of recognition for your excellent and outstanding record since your coming to these United States, we take great pleasure in awarding to you a full scholarship in Alpha Chapter of Kappa Nu. This scholarship shall be in effect throughout your under graduate days at the University of Rochester.

Henry Sher
President
Alpha Chapter
Kappa Nu

Presented at
Annual Initiation
Banquet, Hotel Rochester
Rochester, N. Y.

showing that I had the required sixteen Regents credits needed to graduate. I even received recognition from the local newspapers. That accomplishment enabled me to apply to the University of Rochester where I was accepted and given a scholarship. Thus, after arriving here in the summer of 1947, I had learned enough English to get by, had graduated from high school, and was about to become a full-time college student in the late summer of 1948, Class of 1952.

What would it be like to be dropped off on the moon or some other strange planet? Similarly, what was it like to go from the forests of Poland by way of a displaced persons' camp in Italy, with just a meager knowledge of the English language, to the University of Rochester in just one year? For one thing, it was very scary.

Although I had managed to learn enough English to get through high school, I was hardly prepared to become a full-time student at the University of Rochester. I was anxious but very excited. I had to practically pinch myself in order to believe that I was where I was. The remainder of my family, my two sisters and brother, were very proud of me. Knowing that I had no money, Feitche immediately began to send me a few dollars whenever she could. She and Shleime were newcomers to Mexico and had practically nothing, yet she saved $2.00 or $5.00 from her weekly or biweekly grocery money and sent it to me so that I might pursue my dream. My benefactor during my first year in Rochester, Noah Sher, did not forget me either. He offered to let me work in the warehouse whenever I had vacation time, and he continued to give me gifts from time-to-time.

At school I was assigned a room in Burton Hall, right off the quadrangle. I could see and feel the pulse of the university, alive and bustling with eager young men and women in pursuit of learning.

Before too long I became acquainted with a number of schoolmates, some sophomores, juniors, and seniors who belonged to a Jewish fraternity called Kappa Nu. Before the year was out, I was invited to join, given a scholarship and awarded membership in the fraternity. To some extent Kappa Nu became my new "family."

Coming after years of indescribable horrors, loss of loved ones, forced separation from remaining family members, and uprooting, the calm of life on campus was almost unreal. My four years at the University of Rochester turned out to be by far the best years of my life. I loved my friends, loved school, loved to learn, and appreciated life.

Berl is in the third row down, second from left.

With a view towards law school, I elected history as my major and psychology as a minor. I was fortunate to have several outstanding professors, including Dexter Perkins and Arthur J. May. They made the study of history fun.

My fraternity brothers made sure I felt included and involved. They helped me to learn aspects of the English language that one does not learn from books or in a classroom. They also taught me the art of dating, of which I knew nothing. When short vacations came, one or the other of my fraternity brothers would invite me to go home with him. I fondly recall the great time with Sal Becker at his home in Salem, Massachusetts. His family celebrated Passover in a way that reminded me of holidays at my home in Jasionowka.

Many other school friends contributed to the enjoyment of my years at the U of R. Several of my fraternity brothers deserve special mention: Ted (Amdursky) Anders, who became a pediatrician and now lives in Rockville, Maryland. Ted and his wife Mim remain very dear to me. Jerry Rotenberg, who is now a Certified Public Accountant in Rochester. Gerald Davidson, now a divorce lawyer in Rochester. Irving Geldin, who was a psychologist and died some years ago.

Although I had a U of R scholarship, I needed to earn money to pay for room, board, books, and so forth. One of my friends told me about the hotels in the Catskill Mountains where a waiter could earn and save $1,500 to $2,000 in a summer. This friend helped me find a job in a small hotel near Liberty, New York. There I started as a busboy and was soon promoted to waiter. The next summer I was hired by the Woodley Hotel, near Ellenville, New York, as a waiter, promoted to head waiter, and the following season to manager. I worked there four summers and made enough money each summer to survive the following school year.

After my first year at the University of Rochester, I began to feel more self-assured, although insecurity continued to plague me for years to come. I began to develop a social life. I played cards, spent summer afternoons canoeing on the Genesee River, and began to date. Life was very full and very pleasant. During my last year at the University of Rochester, my continued insecurity drove me to apply to seven law schools: Harvard, Yale, Michigan, Chicago, Cornell, Columbia, and NYU. You can imagine my amazement when I received seven acceptances! I then wrote to all the schools asking for a scholarship. Again, to my amazement, all seven schools offered me scholarships, the largest from Cornell and the smallest from Harvard. Lawyer friends whom I consulted all advised me to go to Harvard even if I ended up borrowing money.

My three years at Harvard Law School were satisfactory. The work was hard and competition keen. After one year in the dorm, I and five other law students rented a large house within walking distance of the school. With my experience of five years in the Catskill Mountains, I was a pretty good cook. We made a deal—the others would pay for all the food and do the cleaning, and I would cook dinner seven days a week. I always prepared food for ten or more since dates and other drop-ins often graced our table.

My housemates were brilliant individuals and outstanding in many ways. One, Donald Schwartz, a very dear friend, went on to become a professor of law and a recognized authority in the field of corporate responsibility. Unfortunately, he died a number of years ago. Herbert L. Hiller was an outstanding housemate who now lives in Georgetown, Florida. He is a writer and travel expert and has written many guide books. Arthur H. Rosenfeldt, another brilliant housemate and friend, went on to become counsel to a large publishing house.

Another classmate, although not a housemate, was my friend Wilmer J. Patlow. Wilmer was a Rochester native. He was brilliant and possessed a great sense of humor. Wilmer needed a job badly, and I took him with me to the Catskill Mountains where I gave him a job waiting in the children's dining room. Wilmer eventually became a justice of the New York State Supreme Court. He died several years ago, and to this day I miss him very much.

One friendship that developed during my days at the University of Rochester, enriched my life more than any other. To this day my friend Jules Cohen and his wife Doris are much more than just friends. Jules was a classmate and went on to become a cardiologist and, in recent years, the Dean of Education at the University of Rochester Medical School. He and Doris have made a substantial difference in my family's life.

Other friends, too, have made an important difference in my life: Elaine and Leonard Simon, Rabbi Herbert Bronstein and his wife, Tamar; Dr. Charles DeMarco and his wife, Marie; Earl Wensel and his wife, Ginny. Their children, Andrew and Benjamin, "adopted" Jane and me as grandparents. They remain part of our extended family; Margie Baker Price and her children who "elected" Jane and me as godparents; Len Freedman and his late wife, Ann Weiss, who tragically died while very young and full of life; several families who were part of a *chavurah* which greatly enriched our lives. Although the *chavurah* no longer exists, the friendships remain.

For many years, and to this day, I meet almost every morning for coffee with several friends with whom I deal professionally as well. Three of them, Gordon Malboeuf, Ron Staub and Frank Casaceli have played a part in making me look forward to the days in the office. During the twenty or so minutes we spend together over coffee, we resolve all the world's problems, listen to each other's concerns, and, after some twenty years of getting together, "fight" over whose turn it is to pay. Once, when I was visiting Australia, my coffee buddies sent me a fax saying that it was Wednesday and my turn to pay. They faxed me the bill, too, for $5.42. Of course, in return I faxed them a $100 bill requesting that they send me back the change. I am still waiting. I will always be grateful to those of my friends I have mentioned and others too numerous to mention.

While at Harvard I came back to Rochester for vacation, and there I met your grandma, Jane Moress. She was a long way from being a grandma then, and I loved her from the start. Because I had two years of school before graduation, Grandma Jane and I corresponded and visited whenever possible. We were married on July 3, 1955, soon after I graduated.

Grandma Jane was all I ever dreamed of—lovely, intelligent, sensitive, and understanding. She offered so much more than I, an insecure survivor of the Holocaust, could hope for. Her family accepted me, and before long I looked at them as my family. Grandma Jane and I have been married for over forty years. She is my wife, confidante, and friend. After all these years, I can still say and mean:

אני לדודי ודודי לי

I am my beloved's and my beloved is mine.

Before graduating from Harvard, I applied for a job with Marvin R. Dye of the New York State Court of Appeals. I got the job, and although the work was demanding and difficult, I loved it. When the court was in session, I was in Albany working twelve- to fifteen-hour days and not minding it. The judges of the Court of Appeals were decent human beings, and Judge Dye was especially kind and nice to work for. I also had the opportunity to get to know the other clerks, including Mario Cuomo who was then clerking for Judge Burke.

In 1958, after 2 1/2 years with the Court of Appeals, I took a job with a Rochester lawyer, Francis L. Claus, and in 1961 we formed a partnership that still functions to this day. Claus died in 1971, and just about at that time, we hired a young lawyer, Frank A. Schwartzman. He was soon given a partnership interest, and we remain partners to this day. Frank is one of the finest, most decent individuals I have ever known. In the twenty-five years we have worked together, we have never had a serious disagreement. Now that I am getting on in age and my energies are diminishing, I appreciate Frank's help and devotion more than ever.

The Daily Record.

Western New York's Business and Legal Newspaper

Vol. 49, No. 50 | Phone BAker 5-7540 | Rochester, N. Y., Thursday, March 13, 1958 | Phone BAker 5-7540 | Fifteen Cents

JOINS LAW FIRM — Bernard Schuster, 29, former clerk to Associate Judge Marvin R. Dye of the State Court of Appeals, has joined the Francis L. Claus law office, 619 Powers Bldg. A graduate of Harvard Law School, Schuster is a member of the Rochester and New York State Bar Assns. He resides with his wife at 24 North Goodman St. His new office phone number is LO 2-6250.

As I look back at my career of forty years, I regret little. True, I will not be remembered as Clarence Darrow. I did not seek fame and did not sell my soul for the sake of a great fortune. Yet, with all humility, I can say that I have no regrets. For forty years I have tried to live and practice within the letter of the law. I have helped many thousands of people and have always done my best. I have treated people fairly with compassion and understanding. The fact that someone could not pay for services never prevented me from helping them. In forty years of practice no client has ever filed a grievance or complaint against me. Over the years, thousands have sent me notes expressing their thanks and gratitude. That for me was and remains reward enough.

The Daily Record.

Vol. 52, No. 128 Phone BAker 5-7540 Rochester, N. Y., Wednesday, July 5, 1961 Phone BAker 5-7549 Fifteen Cents

FRANCIS L. CLAUS WILLARD P. CURRY BERNARD SCHUSTER

Lawyers Form Firm; 2 Become Partners

Formation of a new law firm and the addition of new partners to two established firms were announced at midyear.

Francis L. Claus, Willard P. Curry and Bernard Schuster has formed a partnership under the firm name of Claus, Curry & Schuster with offices at 619 Powers Bldg.

James W. Richards, 34, has been made a partner of MacFarlane, Harris, Martin, Kendall & Dutcher.

Bruce E. Hansen, 34, has been made a partner of Strang, Wright, Combs, Wiser & Shaw.

Claus, a graduate of Niagara University, first practiced public accounting and was co-author of the Federal Redbook and Practice Manual. He was admitted to the bar in 1943 and was a partner in the firm of Claus & Meagher until Thomas J. Meagher became Children's Court judge and the partnership ended.

Curry was born in Ontario, Canada and attended primary school there. He was graduated from Genesee Wesley Seminary and Albany Law School and was admitted to practice in 1924.

Schuster, born in Poland, came to the U. S. in 1947. He was graduated from the University of Rochester and Harvard Law School, then, in 1955, became clerk to Court of Appeals Judge Marvin R. Dye.

Richards, a graduate of Union College and Albany Law School, was admitted to the bar and the U. S. Army in 1954. In 1956 he became asociated with the MacFarlane, Harris firm. Two years later he began operating the firm's branch office in Rush.

Hansen, native of Albany, was graduated from State University, College of Education at Albany and Albany Law School. He joined the Strang firm in 1952 immediately after being admited to the bar. He served in the Navy during World War II.

My chosen career has been rewarding in many ways. Concentrating in estate, real estate, and tax work brought me many fine and often very interesting clients. I could, and perhaps will someday, write a book just telling tales about the unusual clients I have represented. One elderly lady who lived in a run-down apartment in a poor section of the city one day called to ask if I could come to see her concerning a will she would like to have me draw, saying that it was difficult for her to get to our office. To my amazement, I found that she was worth about two million dollars. Her husband had been a controller for Kodak and had left her a lot of stock. She had a son who, after divorcing his first wife, went to Germany married a woman there and became the local Nazi leader. When my client died some years later, she left all her money to two grand daughters who lived out of town. They kept asking me, "Why did grandma leave us anything when we never paid any attention to her?"

Many of the clients I still represent have been clients of mine for 20, 30, or even 40 years. Just a few months ago a great lady died, one day before her 98th birthday. She and her late husband, who had died some ten years earlier, owned a house in the city and a beautiful 105 acre farm some

50 miles outside of Rochester. After her husband died my client moved to the farm where she could enjoy the beautiful landscape, the pond filled with fish, the lake which could be seen from some parts of her property, and the peace and quiet. Several years ago we decided to sell her house in the city. I hired a woman to sell what I thought was mostly junk cluttering every room in the house, the attic, and basement. Imagine my surprise when that "junk" brought in over $70,000, more than the value of the house itself.

This wonderful lady desperately wanted to live to her 100th birthday. Not too long before she died, during one of my monthly visits to her farm, she told me that she wanted me to start planning her 100th birthday party, and without hesitation I promised to do so.

Yes, I have been lucky to have had a fine career, a good practice rewarding in all sorts of ways. Even now, when I could well afford to retire, I still come to the office by 7 a.m. most days simply because I enjoy doing what I'm doing and always wait for the next unusual client who might need my help. My work did not prevent me from giving my time and energies to various organizations and causes. Over the years I have served on the boards of Temple Brith Kodesh, Hillel School, The Jewish Community Federation, The Jewish Community Center, The Bureau of Jewish Education, The Jewish Family Service, the Holocaust Museum Commission, and others. I taught Sunday school for many years, lectured at the University of Rochester in a course on the Holocaust, and have undertaken many other community obligations. I have many wonderful memories and hopefully new challenges to look forward to.

You know that Grandma Jane and I were blessed with three children, Deborah, Jamie, and Miriam. I will not write too much concerning them. You—Rachel, Sarah, Saul, Christy and Laura—can get all the details from your parents concerning their stories, their searches, and their travels through childhood, youth, and adult life. Each in his or her way enriched my life and gave me much joy. They gave me you, my beloved grandchildren, and that is what I treasure most.

Picture taken in Melbourne, Australia December 1974 — Wedding of Marilyn & Harry Burstein

1. *Berl Schuster*
2. *Michael Schwartz - husband of my niece Roske (9)*
3. *My brother Maishe Schuster*
4. *Shleime Schuster - cousin & brother-in-law*
5. *Tony Shalit - husband of my niece Suzanne (13)*
6. *Mark Schwartz - son of Roske (9)*
7. *Fay Schwartz Cohen - daughter of Roske (9)*
8. *My sister Baile Gunn*
9. *My niece Roske Schwartz*
10. *Marilyn Schwartz - daughter of Roske (9)*
11. *My brother Maishe's wife Modelein Schuster*
12. *My sister Feitche*
13. *My niece Suzanne Shalit*
14. *Relative of groom*
15. *Relative of groom*
16. *Maishe's son Jamie Schuster (3)*
17. *Roske's (9) son, Andrew Schwartz*

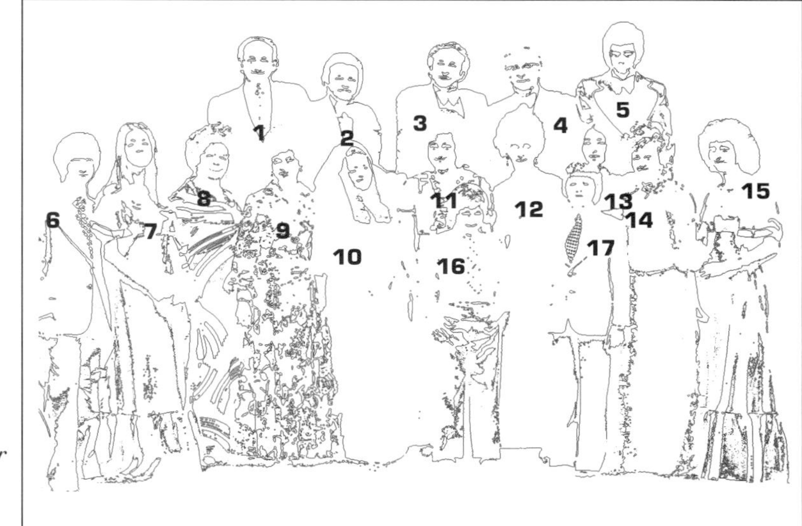

REFLECTIONS AND HOPES

What has my life, with all its trials and tribulations, taught me? What, if anything, can I pass on to you, my dearest grandchildren? Having survived the Holocaust years, I was determined to do whatever I could to help make this world a better place. I have not been in a position to help do away with man's inhumanity to man. Wars continue to plague us. Hatred and strife have lifted their ugly heads again and again. We are as yet not turning our swords into plowshares and have yet to come to love our neighbors as ourselves. Still, I feel that you, my grandchildren, will continue to make progress toward making this world a better place for you and the generations to follow. I hope you will never stop trying to do so.

Individually, I have tried to help as many people as I could. I have tried to listen to people and to give of my time and energies so that their pain, fears, and troubles might be diminished.

Have I achieved all that I might have? Not likely. Have my attempts been wasted? Not at all. Bessie Anderson Stanley set forth what she considered a successful life. She writes:

"He has achieved success
who has lived well,
laughed often and loved much;
who has enjoyed...
the respect of intelligent men
and the love of children;
who has filled his niche
and accomplished his task;
who has left the world better
than he found it...
who never lacked appreciation
of earth's beauty
or failed to express it;
who has always looked for
the best in others
and gave them the best he had..."

It is my hope that you, my loved ones, will feel that my life has truly been successful. It is my further hope that you will strive to set such goals for yourselves that will allow you to succeed.

I hope that you will love yourselves and the people near and dear to you; that you will help others and make the world a better place for all living beings. We live in a beautiful world, and each one of us has an opportunity and the responsibility to conduct our lives in such a way as to enhance its beauty.

It is my hope that I will continue to live on to tell my stories to your children, and that someday your children will say, "Great Grandpa Berl, tell me about when you were a little boy." Should I not be around to tell these stories, I will count on you to tell my story to your children and grandchildren and to carry the Schuster legacy from generation to generation.

A few words from Grandma Jane

Now, it is my turn to contribute to the telling of Grandpa Bernie's story. As I write this, it is September 13, 1996, or Erev Rosh HaShanah, 5756, the birthday of the world. It is a time of looking backward and forward at once. One month ago, Saul Benjamin had a birthday. In about a week, on September 22, Erev Yom Kippur, it will be Great Grandpa Saul's birthday, who would be 94 years old if he were alive. It is a time to remember, and that is what Grandpa Bernie has been doing in these memoirs.

The story has been told, but, like the world, it is not yet complete. There is more to come, more birthdays, more laughter, more tears, more sharing of love, more living each day as the gift it is. To celebrate the gift of Grandpa Bernie's sharing his life with mine, in June 1990, I wrote the following tribute and entered it into a contest about "Unsung Heroes." I never heard from them, but that is all right. The main thing is, Grandpa Bernie truly is a hero, and everyone who knows him even a little, knows this to be true. And now, with Grandpa's memoirs in hand, and my words that follow, he is no longer unsung. May he continue to make music and harmony among us for many, many years.

With love, in love,

Grandma Jane

Jane Moress Schuster

MY UNSUNG HERO:
BERNIE (BERL) SCHUSTER

Bernie could have become bitter and vengeful at any time: as a child, living in a Jewish shtetl in the midst of a largely hostile Poland, watching his family build a shelter that would be no shelter from the Nazis; as a twelve-year-old holding his dying father in his arms; as a teen-ager hiding in barns or the forest; or at any time afterwards. He could have, but didn't.

Bernie in 1955

Instead he remained an idealist, leading on foot groups of other survivors over the mountains into Italy where they found welcome respite on their journey to the homeland—Palestine, now Israel. He himself accepted his aunt's invitation to come to America. Romantic and hopelessly in love with life, he caught a freighter, learning English on shipboard as he listened to meal announcements and the popular songs of the day. He wrote love poems in Yiddish and sketched pictures between bouts of seasickness. He arrived in New York, his promised land, in 1947, at the age of 19. Years later, he would remark wistfully that he wished he still had the cardboard suitcase that had held all his possessions then, as well as the thirty-seven cents he had had in his pocket.

These, his hope, and the loving welcome of cousins, softened the twin blows to his vanity of a haircut that removed his long curls and the dental work necessary to replace teeth rotted by lack of food and care. These trials were soon followed by a hard choice: to accede to his family's demand that he take over their thriving meat-packing business; or, his schooling having been cut off at age 12, to go to school and become what he dreamed of being—a lawyer. He chose the latter, refusing to surrender to his family's skepticism about his ability to achieve his goal when he didn't yet speak English. He found a room and a job in a warehouse where his boss ordered him to lie down and nap on the crates so he could stay awake for his high school classes at night. In one year, he covered all four years of high school, then went on to university study before attending law school. Summers he spent working in the Catskill Mountains to earn enough money to carry him through the school years.

After graduating from law school, he served for several years as clerk for a judge on New York State's highest court, the Court of Appeals. This experience confirmed his sense of the value of a system based on law and decency. Having known the chaos and terror of tyranny, he basked in the freedom and justice he found in the United States. Having seen the most fundamental indignities and callousnesses inflicted on individuals, he cherished this country's insistence on individual liberty within a compassionate society. He became what he remains, a staunch supporter of the constitutional basis of our democracy.

Our wedding day.

He married and had three children, treating his wife and offspring with characteristic love and tenderness. He is still with the small law firm he joined then. He and his partners maintain a lifetime association based on mutual love and trust.

In a changing world, he has remained unchanged, mourning the world's growing indifference and complexity as he steadily responds with dependable concern and kindness to all who need him. Where other lawyers charge by the phone call on computerized time-tracking systems, he does the unheard of, making "house calls" to the lonely, ill, or housebound. Instead of counting minutes, he spends unpaid hours with those whom life has wounded. He values the talents of others and generously barters his skills in financial management with craftsmen and others. He counts among his devoted friends a number of people who own homes and businesses they would have lost were it not for his help. He used to go every week to one profligate friend's gas station to empty his pockets of cash, applying it for him to his debts.

He might have become bitter and reveled egotistically in the wealth this country offered. Instead, he "plowed" whatever he saved into the future, into his children and into the land. His heart stayed soft as his hands became calloused with the labor of turning a few acres in the countryside into a haven for wildlife and humans alike. He has planted hundreds of trees, shrubs, and flowers, although he has, sadly, not managed to attract the hummingbirds he longs to see. He has dug a pond and saved acres of woods from destruction by grape vines. He has lugged out rusting debris and marked trails in the woods. He has even built an outhouse, putting it together in the garage of his suburban home, to the surprised comments of neighbors, before trucking it to the woods. This he did for his wife, who balked at anything more rustic. In this way, he coaxed her into sharing this part of his life as he has coaxed life into returning to him what he has offered to the world: good humor, passion, compassion, and reverence for all things living. From death, he has built a life, not only for himself, but for those he loves, creating a circle of love around him that extends to as much of the planet as he can reach.

He bought himself his first new vehicle this year—a red four-wheel-drive truck. His delight in this reflects his spirit. He bought it to keep from becoming mired in the mud that he often has to pass to get from the driveway to his land. Always in life he has found a way to keep from sinking into the mud that lay along his path. Always he has found a way for himself and those he loves and those who love him to get where they needed to go. Once on dry land himself, he has always gone back to help others, whether survivors from Poland going to Italy, his friends whose genius lies in areas other than management, his wife who bases her explorations into life on the bedrock of his devotion, or his children and grandchildren whose lives he nurtures. Wherever he goes or whomever he touches, he leaves behind an indelible memory, his smile. Children cuddle in his embrace. A man of his word, his whole being is an offering, a thanksgiving for blessings received, blessings which he in turn bestows on all who know him.

June, 1990

Our house on Colonia Street as it looked in 1992

Colonia Street — where I lived 1932-1945

My brother Maishe — 1992

Our yard in 1992

Above and below: Kotowizna Street now known as Miunoma where I lived until about age four.

The church and church wall in Jasionowka.

Afterword

Rochester, N.Y., Thursday, December 26, 1996

The Daily Record

Today's Quotation

"Everything is in a state of flux, including the status quo."
— Robert Byrne

Second Class Postage Paid at Rochester, NY

Monroe County's Business/Legal Daily Newspaper

$1.00

The Daily Record

Rochester Attorney Pens His Memoirs of the Holocaust

As a young child growing up in Poland, Rochester attorney Bernard Schuster was confronted with the horrors of the Holocaust. The youngest of eight children, Schuster was forced to witness the torture and deaths of his parents, several siblings and virtually his entire town.

Now in his sixties, Schuster wanted to find a way to chronicle his story to preserve this bittersweet heritage for his children, grandchildren and for future generations of his family.

The process of writing his memoirs proved to be a little more complicated than you might think. Schuster was plagued by amnesia and further confronted by the inability to verify events or dates with his parents or siblings and the pain of having to relive the experiences over and over again.

"As I write this, I am past 65 years of age and the recollections I search for happened long, long ago and far away. I am no longer sure that what I think I recollect actually happened as I remember. I think it is possible to repress some memories which are painful and "edit" recollections in order to help us cope," he said.

Bernard Schuster

The title of his memoirs, *I Will Die Tomorrow, But Not Today* reflects the advice Schuster received from a young Polish farm woman while he hid in her barn. That philosophy served him well during the four years of escape from the Nazis.

After leaving Poland, Schuster helped others escape to Palestine before moving to live in the United States with an aunt. Without knowing a single word of English and having missed out on most of his schooling, Schuster completed four years of high school in night school, while working full-time during the day. He went on to obtain a complete scholarship at the University of Rochester and graduated from Harvard Law School.

As an attorney for the last 41 years, Schuster had the rare privilege of being selected as a clerk for the New York State Court of Appeals before forming the firm Claus, Curry, Schuster and Schwartzman.

"For 40 years I have tried to live and practice within the letter of the law. I have helped many thousands of people and have always done my best. I have treated people fairly, with compassion and understanding. The fact that someone could not pay for services never prevented me from helping them," he said.

Today, Schuster remains an active community volunteer who serves on the boards of the Jewish Community Center, Jewish Family Service, the Holocaust Commission, etc.

His memoirs have been published along with a journal penned by Schuster's late sister, Feitche, between 1939 and 1945. Together, these two documents give the community a glance at what transpired during the Holocaust.

ROCHESTER

living

DEMOCRAT AND CHRONICLE / TIMES-UNION

C SECTION

Friday
entertainment

'SubUrbia' tries to be 'American Graffiti' for today's twentysomethings. It falls short.
Turn to Page 3C.

ANNETTE LEIN staff photographer

His story *Bernard Schuster, at the JCC's Holocaust Memorial, has written his memoirs and wants other survivors to do the same.*

LOOK BACK IN SORROW

Brighton survivor shares his story of living past the Holocaust

BY STAFF WRITER
DEBORAH FINEBLUM RAUB

In the course of four days, Bernard Schuster's father has frozen to death in his arms. His mother and little sister have been shot before his eyes. So the 14-year-old is trudging back to town to surrender to the Germans and certain death when a woman stops him.

Her husband is an anti-Semite, she tells him, but she will hide the boy in the barn and slip him food and bacon grease to rub on his frostbite.

And she tells him, "Every day, remember to say to yourself, 'I may die tomorrow, but not today.' "

The date is Jan. 30, 1943, the place Jasionowka (Ya-shen-OUF-kah), Poland. And the stranger's words have given Schuster the mantra that will preserve him through the pain, hunger, fear and lice that will plague him for two long years until he is liberated.

Now, a half century later and thousands of miles away in the parallel universe of Rochester, N.Y., Schuster has repeated these words once more, as the title of a book about his ordeal.

SCHUSTER, PAGE **8C**

Family heirlooms
Bernard Schuster, at age 4 (above), and his parents and siblings circa 1920, eight years before Schuster was born.

Schuster

FROM PAGE 1C

The gentle, jovial Brighton grandfather and lawyer will mark his 69th birthday this month. He'll do so amid appointments with clients, visits with grandchildren and occasional escapes with his wife, Jane, to their weekend farm in Victor.

But as one of about a half-million Jews who lived through the Holocaust, Schuster rarely mentioned those years to his three children as they were growing up.

"Like other survivors, I had a guilty feeling," he recalls. "I wondered why I survived and better people didn't. My brother Maier was brilliant and good and he didn't survive."

Then, 20 years ago, Rabbi Abraham Karp asked Schuster to share his history with Karp's class at the University of Rochester.

Soon Schuster was speaking to high-schoolers and to other college classes. Before long, his own children came to hear their father talk about his experiences.

And when granddaughter Sarah Schuster, now 8, begged him to "tell me about when you were a little boy," he began, slowly, to talk to her about growing up in Poland. Her favorite: the day he got a spanking for ruining his new Passover suit in the mud.

"Telling her these stories, I realized I needed to set down my story for my grandchildren. It was time to do that."

And what a story it is: a tale of survival against all odds, and one that Schuster will share again Sunday on Yom Hashoah, Holocaust Memorial Day.

Although 75 percent of the 2,000 souls in his home village were Jews, anti-Semitism was as familiar to the eight Schuster children as the cow in their backyard. "Ours was a little island in a sea of hate," Schuster recalls. Market day brought surrounding farmers to town to trade their eggs and chickens for the candles and shoes the Jews sold. Inevitably a few of the visitors would get drunk at night and "have a little fun" beating up Jews and burning their homes.

Each Easter week also meant attacks on the "Christ killers," and each Passover renewed allegations that Jews were using the blood of Christian children in the holiday matzos. "Yes, we always lived in fear," remembers Schuster.

Family gathering *This1920 photo shows many of Schuster's relatives — most of whom died in the Holocaust.*

> *"Like other survivors, I had a guilty feeling. I wondered why I survived and better people didn't. My brother Maier was brilliant and good and he didn't survive."*
>
> **BERNARD SCHUSTER**

Happier times *Schuster's brother Maier (front) was among those who died; sister Feitche (center) kept a wartime diary.*

were using the blood of Christian children in the holiday matzos. "Yes, we always lived in fear," remembers Schuster.

Things got worse in September 1939, when he was 11 and war broke out. But life for Polish Jews became "pure hell," he says, on June 21, 1941, when the Russians turned that part of Poland over to Germany. And the Nazis had plenty of help from Poles who carried out attacks on Jews with chilling enthusiasm.

Still, Schuster insists without a trace of irony, "we were a lucky town." As one of the last in the region to be "liquidated," Jasionowka had already received an influx of Jews from neighboring towns seeking shelter — "and warning us what to expect."

One Sunday morning, a group of Polish youths beat Schuster's father and threw him into a creek, blinding him in one eye. When his children discovered him, he begged them to let him die. But they took him home to nurse him back to health, which he was never to regain.

On Jan. 25, 1943, when Jasionowka was liquidated, cars with loudspeakers barked orders for all Jews to report to the center of town or risk being shot on sight. But the Schuster family moved to the hiding place above their backyard tannery. Some people with small children, however, did report to the Germans, for fear that their babies would make noise and trigger discovery. None of them ever returned.

Soon, with the remaining family members in danger of freezing to death, Schuster and his weakened father ventured out, camouflaged against the snow under bed sheets, to seek a hiding place in the woods. From there they watched helplessly as Schuster's mother and 10-year-old sister, Tzipe, were gunned down.

With nowhere to turn, Schuster and his father appealed to a neighboring farmer they'd paid to help them. He now refused, and Schuster's father froze to death.

That's when Schuster resigned himself to the German roundup — and when his rescuer, Mrs. Czarniecki, hid him in her barn.

There he stayed for two months, watching the antics of the farm children and animals through a crack in the wall. Many a night he helped himself to the pigs' slop and made peace with the mice with whom he shared his quarters.

When two other Jewish boys came looking for sanctuary, Schuster joined them and, with another teen, forged a foursome who would remain together, stealing whatever food they could and hiding in a bunker they'd dug in the forest, for the two remaining years of the war.

At liberation, Schuster feared he'd discover no other family members still alive, but he was relieved to find two sisters, a brother and some cousins. They were among the 82 of the town's 1,500 Jews who survived.

Still, their troubles were far from over. A group of Poles "set out to finish the job Hitler started," going from house to house killing Jews. This time, however, the Schusters were ready — with guns and grenades. When some Poles set out to torch their house, Schuster's brother lobbed a grenade and they retreated. But the attack made the family realize that the "liberation" had in no way ended the war against Poland's Jews.

The family bid farewell to Jasionowka forever, seeking sanctuary with the town's other remaining Jews in the nearest city, Bialystok. From there, Schuster led a group of survivors through Czechoslovakia, Hungary, Austria and Germany to Italy, where they hoped to book passage to Palestine.

But while scrambling illegally over a border, Schuster was shot in the arm and stomach by a guard. While recuperating in a hospital in Italy, his aunt Mary Kaufman caught up with him, sending him a ticket for travel to her home city of Rochester.

He was given a visa only because, at 19, he was still a minor by the standards of the day. His sisters and brother, who were over 21, weren't welcomed by the United States and eventually found homes in Australia and Mexico.

Arriving in Rochester in spring 1947, Schuster finished East Evening High School on Alexander Street in just one year, while working by day in a warehouse. He then completed the University of Rochester and story by a man named Elie Wiesel makes it real and refutes all the revisionism. I'm not trying to compare myself to them, but one book about a real person's experiences has real impact."

In addition to the book and his classroom presentations, Schuster is one of 40 local survivors to record oral histories for movie director Steven Spielberg's Shoah Project. He's also served as chairman of the local Jewish Community Federation's Center for Holocaust Awareness and Information (CHAI), co-chaired the Auschwitz exhibit at Monroe Community College 10 years ago and worked with MCC's Holocaust and Genocide Project.

He's donated 198 copies of his book, *I May Die Tomorrow, But Not Today*, to CHAI to help raise funds for educational programs.

The volume also includes the wartime diary of Schuster's older sister Feitche, who lived in Mexico until her death 10 years ago and is buried in Israel.

"It is our own autumn," she wrote. "We are all dying, surrounded by a world of strangers."

A half century later, her little brother says quietly:

"It's given me a great deal of satisfaction, knowing that I am doing my part to document this, not just for my family, but for history. And for the 6 million people who were led into gas chambers and trenches. In my little way, I'm doing my part." ❑

For information on obtaining copies of Bernard Schuster's book, I May Die Tomorrow, But Not Today, *call the Jewish Community Federation's Center for Holocaust Awareness and Information at (716) 461-0290.*

VOL. LXX, NO. 40 ■ ROCHESTER, N.Y. ■ APRIL 15, 1993 ■ NISSAN 24, 5753 ■ $18 per year within Monroe County, $20 outside county ■ 50¢ per issue

YOM HASHOAH FEATURE

A Survivor's Recollections

BY MALINDA BRENT

Following is an interview with Bernard Schuster, a survivor of the Holocaust. Slightly edited for publishing, its integrity as the vivid recollection of a Polish Jew struggling to survive during Nazi occupation remains intact. In order to stay alive during World War II, Schuster and two companions spent two years hiding underground in a makeshift bunker in the "Black Forest" in Poland.

In 1947, Schuster made his way to Rochester. After graduating Harvard Law School, he has been a partner of the firm Claus, Curry, Schuster & Schwartzman since the 1950s. In his early '60s now, he lives with his wife Jane at their home in Brighton.

When it came to Rochester in 1987, Schuster was chairman of the Auschwitz Exhibit. Also, as chairman of the Holocaust Commission in Rochester for several years, he has organized many services for Holocaust Memorial Day. This year, however, he will be visiting relatives in Israel on that day. A soft-spoken man with a persistent Eastern European accent, bright eyes and a gentle smile, he has a quiet, unassuming manner.

An Interview: BERNARD SCHUSTER

Q: **Is It difficult for you to talk about your experience?**

A: It is hard speaking about those experiences. For many years, I have done so, nevertheless, because I feel that if people like myself who still remember what happened don't convey the message, who's going to do so? So, consequently, for the past 17 years or so, I was a guest lecturer at the University of Rochester in Dr. Karp's course on the Holocaust which he was teaching. I have also spoken at many other places, high schools, various gatherings, the Auschwitz Exhibit when it came here to Rochester — I was chairman of that. I feel that no matter how painful it is, we must talk about it, especially since there are already so-called "revisionists" who are claiming that the Holocaust never happened. Obviously it happened.

Q: **How can you bear to hear that?**

A: It isn't easy. It's difficult really. You say to yourself "How can they be so stupid or so vicious as to claim that it never happened?" What happened to my family? What happened to my father, my mother? I came from a family of eight children. What happened to them if the Holocaust never happened? So you have to speak about it.

Q: **Who are these people coming up with these "revisionist" theories?**

A: There are people all over the world who have tried to claim that the Holocaust never happened. Many of them are strictly anti-Semites with a new twist. Many of them are pro-Arab and they have held that the Jews and the leadership of Israel have created the fable of the Holocaust in order to promote world sympathy for the establishment of a state for the Jews in Israel. They claim that is a plot against the Arabs. All kinds of crazy, crazy notions have been woven into this "revisionist" philosophy. Many of them are supposedly intelligent people, professors in universities, and so on, who come out with these horrible tales, and they seem to get away with it. That is why people like myself do have to speak up.

Q: **Would you mind telling me a little bit about your childhood and what happened?**

A: I was born in a little town in eastern Poland. The town is Jashonuvka, a small town like thousands of other small towns in the pale of settlement in Eastern Europe. There were about 2,000 Jews who lived in the town with about 500 Poles. We were surrounded by farms and villages which were all Polish. In 1939, before war broke out, Germany and Russia divided Poland in two halves.

My town fell under Russian occupation, so that actually the war for us, the Holocaust for us, didn't really start until 1941, when Germany invaded Russia. When they came into our town, a few days after June 21, when they attacked the Soviet Union, they burned the whole center of the town down. Unfortunately, our Polish neighbors lined up with the Germans, and they went around pointing out which were Jewish houses. The Germans were using flame-throwers, burning the houses down and shooting people, so that the first morning, the Saturday morning they came into our town, they killed approximately 10 percent of the Jews in our town, about 200 people. From then on, It was just slow torture, day after day, week after week, the Germans would come into town, round up a few young Jewish men usually, make them work a day or two, then make them dig a grave and shoot them. Anybody they caught and took away for a day's work never came back.

This went on until the end of 1942 when we started hearing rumors about concentration camps and crematoriums and gas chambers. They also at that time started liquidating whole communities, claiming that they were relocating them to other areas, but we knew by then that this was not so, that we were being slaughtered on a wholesale scale.

At that time my family made a hiding place above the tannery which my family owned. We built the hiding place so that we could hide out at least for a few days if and when our town was liquidated by the Germans. It was just a horrible period from June 1941 to January 1943.

On January 23, 1943, when the Germans surrounded our town and liquidated our town, they drove everyone to the center of the town for transporting to the gas chambers. Anyone who didn't show up in the center of town and who was found was shot immediately. Part of my family were in hiding at that point, and my father had made arrangements with a Polish farmer who said that if we gave him just about everything we owned, he would hide us out when liquidation takes place. We gave him all of our possessions and goods and we decided to go and reach his farm two at a time from this hiding place.

My father and I were the first two to reach the woods, about a mile away from our house and our tannery. My father and I made it to the forest. My mother and one of my sisters were to come next but were discovered by the Germans as they were walking towards the woods and they were shot. After that we knew that nobody else could come out from the hiding place so my father and I went to the farmer and said "Here we are. Hide us out. Help us." He wouldn't let us in. He wouldn't even give us a piece of bread. He drove us out. We had no place to go. My father and I sat down in the forest and my father actually died of the cold, he froze in the forest.

I was almost frozen also and I decided to go back to town by myself. I was only a youngster at the time. I was born in 1928 and all of this took place in 1943, so I wasn't quite grown up. On the way back to town a Polish farmer's wife saw me. It was a Sunday morning and she asked me where I going. I told her that I was going to town so the Germans could shoot me because it was easier than freezing to death. She took me in and gave me shelter in their barn and she let me hide in the hay in her barn, without her husband's knowledge, because her husband was an anti-Semite and she said he would kill me if he found me. So I was hiding in the barn and she would bring me some food once in a while when she could. She would also bring some medicine because I was frozen and I stayed there for a while.

It must have been about late March or early April when one night I heard knocking on the farm windows in the middle of the night and it was two young men coming to beg for food, and that was my friend, Ruven Degani, and his brother. She told them that I was hiding in the barn. I joined up with them and we lived in the forest from then until we were liberated by the Soviet army at the end of 1944, early 1945, so that is briefly in a nutshell this period.

Bernard as a child.

Living in the forest was not easy. We had no food and no shelter, and we knew that if anyone discovered us, even the Poles, they would kill us or turn us over to the Germans, so we dug a hole in the ground, covered it and made sort of a bunker underground and that's how we lived for two winters and two summers. We had only the clothes on our back and practically no food. Every now and then we would either beg or steal some food in order to survive, or catch what we could in the forest, but in the winter months it was pretty hard to do that, so we were in pretty bad shape. The filth was awful. It was just a horrible situation.

Q: **What happened once the Russians came?**

A: Once the Russians came, we went back to our home town, and to my wonderful amazement, I found that one of my brothers and two of my sisters also survived. They were also hiding with farmers. Also some cousins of mine survived, one of whom is now 87 years old, and who I'm going to visit in Israel, Solomon Schuster. So we all gathered up in his house and decided we would all live there because at that point we heard the Polish people formed an organization dedicated to finishing off the job, killing all the Jews that survived.

Q: **This is after the war was over?**

A: Yes. We knew that they would be coming to kill us even though the Germans were driven out. At that time we armed ourselves with some guns and rifles and grenades. Sure enough, one night, 70 young Polish men came, surrounded the house and tried to kill us. We fought a battle with them most of the night and when they found that they couldn't kill us because we were well-armed, that next morning we left Jashonuvka, never to see it again. I have never been back. At that point, my brother and myself went to the nearest large city and were looking for a way out of Poland, trying to go perhaps to Palestine, as it was known then. We ended up in Italy. We went back and forth because I was helping other people get out of Poland. On one of those trips I was wounded and I ended up in a hospital in Italy. While in the hospital I discovered that I had an aunt in Rochester, New York, who offered to pay for my passage to the United States. My brother and my sister could not come to the United States because there was a very restricted quota, but I could come in under a special provision that was made to take in minors. I was still under 18 years of age. So I was able to come in. I came from Italy to the United States on May 22, 1947.

After I came to Rochester, things changed dramatically for me. I decided to get an education. I was only about 11 years old when the war began, and I had very little education, so I ended up going to East Evening High School, learning English, and taking high school courses at the same time. I worked in a warehouse nine hours a day, loading and unloading bicycles, and then going to night school and studying very hard, but I did manage to do very nicely in high school. I was very fortunate. The assistant principal at the school liked me a lot and took me under his wing. He got permission for me to go from class to class every 15 or 20 minutes so that in one hour I would cover three different courses. In one year I finished my high school education.

I came here in 1947, and in 1948, I entered the University of Rochester, even though I still did not know English very well. After I graduated in 1952, I entered Harvard Law School.

Q: **Does it bother you that much of the world knew what was going on in Eastern Europe but did nothing?**

A: Evidently, the Israelis started dropping people into Germany and Poland to alert people as to what was happening. It is also interesting, when I was chairman of the Auschwitz Exhibit a few years ago, we invited a Polish army general to come here. He had written several books about his experience during the war. He was acting as a courier for the Polish underground and he would be dropped in Poland and then go back to England.

At one point in 1942 he was sent to the United States and a meeting was arranged between him and President Roosevelt. I heard him say that he said to Roosevelt, "Mr. President, the Jews are being exterminated, they are being burned in crematoriums, and they are being gassed. What are you going to do about it?" And he gave him all the details. President Roosevelt unfortunately said, "Well go back and tell them that justice will prevail. We will beat the Germans. They will not win." Mr. Karsky said, "But Mr. President, this is not going to do the millions of Jews who are being slaughtered any good. They are not going to be around to see victory. What can you do for them now?" And Mr. Roosevelt smoked his cigarette through his long cigarette holder and said, "Just tell them justice will prevail."

Bernard Schuster

So everybody knew. Mr. Roosevelt knew. Leaders all over the world knew, but they didn't have

it. They were asked to bomb the railroad tracks that were going back and forth to the gas chambers, and they wouldn't even do that even though they were bombing other parts of Germany and Poland in the same vicinities. This was a low priority for them.

Q: **Aren't you bitter?**

A: Of course I am bitter. We have been bitter. Anyone who has read Eli Weisel's accounts or many others, you cannot help but be bitter. The world was very indifferent. Nobody cared and that's why all these years I have made it a point to care and to speak out, even about the things going on in Bosnia-Herzegovina. I feel that wherever there is injustice, wherever there is in a sense "holocaust," we must take action, we cannot be complacent because those who do not learn from history, as it has been said by someone very famous, are destined to relive it. We have to speak out.

Q: **Do you think that people are learning?**

A: Many times when I would teach, I would be asked by students if I think that a Holocaust could happen again, do I think that it could happen any place in the world? My answer was always unfortunately, "Yes, it could happen again because people just do not care as much as they should." Look at what is happening in many parts of the world, what has happened in South Africa over the years, what is happening in former Yugoslavia. We pay some attention to it, but not enough. Yes, it could happen. There is too much bigotry, too much prejudice. There is just not enough tolerance, and that is very dangerous.

Q: **You would like to think that the world learned something from the Holocaust, but has it? Did it learn and then forget?**

A: I don't know. There was an article in last week's *Jewish Ledger* about the Israelis and the fact that as the generation of the Holocaust is dying out, and those who are still alive are in their 60s and 70s, the young Israelis are now trying to, in a sense, forget much of what happened. They would just as soon trade with Germany now, they feel that enough is enough. We have utilized the Holocaust as a fundraising mechanism, as a justification for some of the things that are going on in Israel, but they can't go on doing that forever. The time has come for the Holocaust to be another horrible chapter in the history of the Jewish people, perhaps more or less like the enslavement in Egypt which we have just remembered on Passover. They feel that perhaps the Holocaust has to be put in its historical perspective as a terrible period, but nevertheless as a historical event, and that we should go on with justifying the existence of Israel as a Jewish state on different basis, on present situations rather than history.

Q: **What sort of advice can you give to younger people as far as preventing it from happening again?**

A: Well, it isn't easy to give advice to younger people. The world is changing, and concerns are different, priorities are different. But one thing I believe remains constant, and that is any prejudice, any intolerance, any indifference is dangerous and can lead to a repetition of the Holocaust in one form or another. That young people should not be concerned entirely with their professions, making a living, their social lives. Nothing is as important as giving of yourself, in seeing to it that the world is a better place for everyone. So long as there are hungry children and children who have no homes, so long as there is prejudice, no one is safe. Young people should do whatever they can to alleviate this.

Q: **Given your experience, does it bother you to see people in the United States buying German products and driving BMWs and Mercedes?**

A: I have mixed feelings about this. I myself would not buy a German product. I realize that on a reasonable basis, there is no reason for that and I have no problem with others buying them. It was over 50 years ago and it's true that Israel owns more Mercedes and BMWs per capita than any other country in the world. But I cannot forget that the German company Krups produced much of the German war machinery during the war as well as material to make the gas chambers. Although I myself do not like to support German industry, I cannot fault others for doing so. ▲

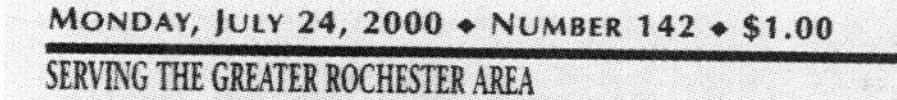

MONDAY, JULY 24, 2000 ◆ NUMBER 142 ◆ $1.00
SERVING THE GREATER ROCHESTER AREA
16 PAGES IN ONE SECTION

THE DAILY RECORD

LAW, REAL ESTATE, FINANCE AND GENERAL INTELLIGENCE SINCE 1908

Bernard Schuster Passes Away

Attorney And Holocaust Survivor Practiced Law In Rochester For 42 Years

BY JILL MILLER

Bernard Schuster, a devoted attorney and Holocaust survivor died Monday, July 17, 2000. He was 72 years-old.

Mr. Schuster spent 42 years practicing law in the Rochester area. He was a partner in Claus, Curry, Schuster & Schwartzman and primarily focused his practice on estate, real estate and tax law.

"He went into the practice of law because he saw it as a helping profession," said Frank Schwartzman, a partner who practiced with Mr. Schuster for over 30 years. "His greatest joy was helping others."

Mr. Schuster was the youngest of eight children, born in Jasionowka, Poland. In 1939, when he was 14, the Nazi's took over his town and he and three others went into hiding in the woods. They dug a whole in the ground and lived there for almost two years. During World War II, Mr. Schuster witnessed the murder of his parents and other family members.

BERNARD SCHUSTER

In 1946 he entered a displaced persons camp in Italy. He also helped other survivors travel to the refugee camps.

A year later, he arrived in Rochester to live with his relatives. He worked in an auto parts warehouse during the day and attended East Evening High School at night. He completed four years of high school in just one year despite not being able to speak English when

See Schuster page 3

Schuster

Continued from page 1

he first arrived in the United States.

He then attended the University of Rochester on a scholarship. In 1952, he was awarded scholarships to seven law schools and chose to attend Harvard Law School. He graduated from Harvard in 1955 and began his law career as a law clerk for Judge Marvin R. Dye of the New York State Court of Appeals, where one of his co-workers was former Gov. Mario Cuomo.

In 1958 he joined Francis Claus and Willard Curry. He became a partner in 1961 and in 1971, the firm changed its name to Claus, Curry, Schuster & Schwartzman.

"His first priority was his family," Schwartzman said. "Then practicing law was the love of his life. He never saw the profession as a business. He very often charged clients what they could afford. If they couldn't afford anything, he would charge nothing."

"My father had an incredibly helping nature," Dr. James Schuster said. "He got a tremendous amount of joy by helping others. He took a legal career and made it into a helping career. I've never met anyone who helped more people."

Mr. Schuster had a lot of elderly clients and was known to make house calls a few times a week.

"His friends became clients and all of his clients became friends," Schwartzman said. "He could relate to a corporate CEO just as easily as he could to a garage mechanic."

In addition to his law practice, Mr. Schuster was also very active in the community. He lectured at Monroe Community College, the University of Rochester, SUNY Brockport, Roberts Wesleyan and local high schools about his personal experience during the war.

"It was a painful process for him, to speak about his experience," Schwartzman said. "Every time he spoke about it he had to re-live it. It would take him a week to get back to normal but he felt it was important to do this and so he rose above it."

Mr. Schuster was interviewed as part of the Steven Spielberg Holocaust oral history project. He also published his memoirs, *I Will Die Tomorrow But Not Today*. Mr. Schuster wrote the book at the urging of family members and dedicated the book to his "parents, brothers and sisters who did survive The Holocaust and whose love and nurturing gave me the strength to survive and tell the story."

In his memoir he wrote, "As I look back at my career of 40 years, I regret little. I have tried to treat people fairly with compassion and understanding. In my 40 years of practice, no client has ever filed a grievance or complaint against me. Over the years, thousands have sent me notes expressing their thanks and gratitude. That for me was and remains reward enough."

"My father had a hard time talking about his experience with my family because it was a painful experience and because of what happened to his family," Dr. Schuster said. "My daughter loved to hear him sing Yiddish lullabies and hear the names of his brothers and sisters. It eventually evolved into her wanting to hear about them. He wrote his memoir so that his children and grandchildren would know his story."

Mr. Schuster was a member of the board of directors of the Jewish Community Center, Jewish Community Federation, Hillel Foundation, University of Rochester, Temple Brith Kodesh, Holocaust Museum Commission, Jewish Family Service, Hillel School and the Advisory Committee of the MCC Holocaust Genocide Studies Project.

"He set a great example for all of us to follow," Schwartzman said.

He was a member of the Monroe County Bar Association where he served on the Managing Partners Committee and the Trusts and Estates Section. He was also a member of the New York State Bar Association.

"He never said no to anyone," Dr. Schuster said. "He helped in whatever way he could. Whether it be through fundraising, or spring planting or helping to set things up for an event — he always did whatever he could."

In his spare time, Mr. Schuster liked to spend time with his family at his 56-acre farm in Victor. The farm has a pond that Mr. Schuster stocked with fish. When someone would catch one, they had to throw it back.

"The farm was another love of his," Schwartzman said. "He built the second home there as a place to share with family and friends."

"The farm was one of his passions," his son said. "He planted trees and created a gorgeous chalet, a place to go to meditate and reflect on nature's beauty."

He is survived by his wife Jane; children Deborah and David Edwards; Dr. James and Jessica Schuster all of Rochester; and Miriam Schuster of Colorado Springs, Colo.; grandchildren, Christina, Laura, Rachel, Sarah and Saul; mother-in-law, Rose Moress Presberg and other family and friends.

"He always had a smile on his face," Dr. Schuster said. "He was incredibly sure about what mattered in life. For him, it was about doing the right thing and making the world a better place and of course his family."

Contributions in Mr. Schuster's memory can be made to Rochester General Hospital for Blood Disorders and Cancer, c/o Dr. Ronald Sham, 1425 Portland Ave., 14621; Temple Sinai, Social Action Committee; or Zachor Fund at the Jewish Community Federation, c/o Barbara Appelbaum; or the Center for Holocaust and Genocide Studies, attention: Sharon Dobkin, Monroe Community College.

TOMORROW

By Jane M. Schuster

Whoever was beaten by this Angel
(who often simply declined the fight)
went away proud and strengthened
and great from that harsh hand,
that kneaded him as if to change his shape.
Winning does not tempt that man.
This is how he grows: by being defeated, decisively,
by constantly greater beings.

R. M. Rilke

After many, many "Todays," each one blessed by Bernie, the day nobody wanted finally came. When it did, Bernie simply took his last breath, at 9:30 A.M. on July 17, 2000, two months to the day after his seventy-second birthday, dying of cancer at home, in our bedroom, his three children and wife at his side.

It is my sacred, sad and self-imposed obligation, as his wife of forty-five years and now his widow of almost one year, to reprint his treasured memoirs and to add to it the end of Bernie's story. But the truth is, the story has not yet ended.

Looking back to that deathbed vigil, I can still see those last moments, moments I relive often. There was that last breath, then silence. My eye was drawn to the light reflected on the shiny transparent tape holding the intravenous feeding tube in place on Bernie's neck. What I remember is how it kept pulsing long after his breathing stopped. His heart—the source of his strength, his forgiveness, his love, what drew people to him, what kept him going, what made him declare so often that he was the luckiest man alive—his heart was that strong.

That heart seems never to have died. Friends' grandchildren keep discovering this book. Out-of-town friends and newly-back-in-touch friends request it. Earl, who wrote and delivered the speech included in this update, feels Bernie's presence every time he goes out to our farm and weeds the raspberries or cuts the grass. Shamans and dancers and cellists go there for what Bernie's presence created, a true sanctuary. This paragraph could go on, but I trust that you, if you knew Bernie, or are meeting him in this book for the first time, will add your own story of Bernie's impact on your life.

You will also encounter Bernie if you go to the Cancer and Blood Disorders Center at the Rochester General Hospital where there is a patients' library corner established with a bequest Bernie made in honor of Dr. Ronald Sham. There will be programs in his memory at the Jewish Community Center of Rochester, Monroe Community College's Holocaust/ Genocide Studies Project, and the Center for Holocaust Awareness and Information (CHAI) of the Jewish Community Federation of Greater Rochester.

And we, the circle of his family and friends, we mourn his loss even as we continue to feel his presence. As soon as we had finished sitting shivah, the required period of mourning in Jewish custom, I took Sarah and Saul, then eleven and eight years old, to a local shop that sells Judaica. They wanted to buy a candlestick to use on Shabbat to honor Bernie's memory. They looked for a long time, finally choosing the one they both agreed was most representative of their grandfather. It is made of four chunky glass blocks stacked on top of each other, alternately green and blue, topped with a clear Lucite holder for the candle. It was one of a pair, and I have the second one on the buffet in my dining room next to the picture of Bernie sitting at his office desk and next to the light I keep lit. Its transparency and colors are like the water in the pond at our farm, where Sarah and Saul loved to go with Bernie. Their candlestick is on the buffet in the dining room of their new home that Bernie did not live to see completed. One of us lights it every Friday night in his memory. And Saul, who loves the Hebrew language and the blessings we say every Friday night, is the keeper of a new tradition started in Bernie's memory—one piece of the challah bread is blessed and taken outdoors to feed the birds. It is a small gesture, but a reminder of a larger presence.

What hurts me the most, almost beyond bearing, is the pain his physical absence has created in his children and grandchildren. How Bernie would have loved to be at Sarah's Bat Mitzvah later this year, to have passed on his knowledge of carpentry and landscaping and so much else to Saul, to have seen Christy, Laura, and Rachel each turn twenty-one years of age. Even a few more years would have made a big difference. But it was not to be.

How Bernie did not want to die! He wanted to live, to continue to serve others, to see my mother through her life cycle, to enjoy the farm, to write more about his life and especially about all the colorful clients he had had and their intriguing escapades, to travel, to see his family in Israel and Australia, and to enjoy his family. Maybe, just maybe, he would have slowed down a bit, but this was dubious so long as he had the energy to keep doing it all.

After his health began to fail him, and treatment for cancer and the cancer itself punished his body, he still pushed himself to go to the office and to maintain his usual schedule. He recovered quickly from prostate surgery in June of 1999. But it was in preparation for that surgery that an abnormality in his white blood cell count was discovered. Diagnosed with a fairly benign form of lymphoma soon after the surgery, he began treatment with oral chemotherapy. Things looked promising through the rest of that summer and fall.

But in December 1999, the lymphoma began to show its true, unpredictable, nasty nature. He had to begin intravenous therapy. Around Passover of 2000, he began to seriously weaken, although even in May things looked very good to Dr. Sham.

By June, he was in the hospital for three weeks as the wonderful doctors and nurses tried to keep ahead of what was devouring him. It was as if they were dealing with a hydra-headed monster, and no matter how many heads they cut off, there were always new ones, and the monster would not die. He came home on June 23 to what was an unspoken hospice situation. His decline was relentless and swift.

As much as any one, it was my mother, Rose Moress Presberg, who helped us through the two major crises of Bernie's last year. When he went in for his surgery in June of 1999, she arranged for private duty nurses around the clock. She said he deserved it, that he'd always been so good to her family, that when we were first married he'd carry my grandfather around, take him to the toilet, and help him in any way he could. What she offered was so much more than simply and generously paying for these nurses. She was in a wheelchair by then and had the services of a devoted and supremely capable nurse, Annie. Yet she let Annie come to the hospital to be with Bernie when she needed her herself. Annie arranged for her sister Cassie and her friend Julie to come also. What we would have done without these and other young, caring, beautiful women I can't begin to imagine.

Then, when Bernie became ill in the spring of 2000, and until he died, these same three women and Annie's mother, Cass, came to be with him every night. My mother again parted with Annie in the afternoons, staying alone in her bedroom. All of this made it possible for Bernie to be at home as he wished. Dependable, conscientious, empathic, they never missed an assigned time.

They kept a written record of what occurred during each of their watches. It is hard to read, hard to recall Bernie's pain and discomfort during those long restless nights and days. Yet it is full, too, of sweet and tender moments.

6:45 A.M. July 1, 2000: Bernie to Annie: Do you know you haven't allowed me one hour's sleep?

Annie: Do you know you're fibbing?

Bernie: Maybe.

6:00 A. M. July 2: Bernie to Julie: You haven't stopped [bugging me] all night.

Julie: That's because I love you.

Bernie: Thanks.

July 3: Bernie to me: This is a beautiful room. It's a good place to recuperate. I feel like going to the farm and planting one thousand trees and picking raspberries, and if I run out of energy, rest for fifteen minutes and go back to work. Does that sound like a sensible plan?

(No record of my response!)

July 14: I lay down next to Bernie and asked: Do you want to kick me out?

Bernie: No! You're my favorite wife!

Where Bernie lay, he could look past the foot of the bed to the wall where we had hung the large, ornately framed photograph of his mother, father and Bernie's five oldest siblings. There is great presence in that picture. His family seemed to be watching over him, even welcoming him into their midst.

I take comfort in that and in what Annie recorded during Bernie's last days. On the night of July 15, two nights before he died, as he slowly drifted into sleep, eyes half-open, Annie records that he said, "Ya, ya, O. K., yup, thank you." A little later he clearly said, "Thank you!" with his eyes closed. Then he put his arms in the air pushing forward, as if to say, Go away!

At 5:00 A. M. Annie wrote: B for the last hour sleeps a few minutes then moves around with unclear mumbling words almost as if he is talking with someone. I try not to always be quick to get his attention because I try to figure out what he is saying and if I do speak to him it's like I'm waking him up and breaking his thoughts.

At 6:08 A. M., Annie added: B reaching left hand smiling towards the door like he sees someone, mumbling a little can't make out any words. I ask Bernie who he sees, he just smiles.

On his final night, the last morning at about 1:00 A. M., I am envious that it is Annie who hears his last words, "It's enough," and who asks him if it's too hard and if he's had enough, and he says "Yes." Then, "I gotta go. I gotta go." And then he lies quietly, eyes wide open, smiling, looks content."

By 7:00 A. M. he lies there "eyes wide open, no facial expression, won't answer at all, breathing different."

By 9:30 A. M. his breath slowed way down, and then stopped.

Somehow this seems almost too personal, too intimate, to share. But in our sanitized culture, where birth and death take place out of sight in some depersonalized institution, we need personal reality. Bernie helped me face my fear of death by his open, heroic struggle and reluctant acceptance of his own mortal end. I feel I owe it to him to share something of his final triumph.

Yes, he died, yes, death took him, but he held on until the last moment, struggling as long as there was hope, then accepting with forbearance untold indignities and assaults, never once railing out or taking out his discomfort on anyone else. If anything, he comforted us. To me, that is triumph, and he is still my hero. More than ever.

Some of the entries in my personal journal during his stay in the hospital speak to who and what Bernie was and what he meant to me and to others:

June 6, 2000: He is giving us all a gift by letting us see how he handles this extreme situation, with what good humor and patience, with how he lets us test ourselves, our limits, our abilities to do what we have never done before, to witness a father in pain and in a life-threatening struggle, to draw close to others, to see how people rise to the occasion, each doing what he or she can: Ginny planting the garden and coming to water it yesterday morning (never mind that it rained hard later), making rice pudding and peanut butter cookies, bringing a vibrant red/pink rhododendron cluster; Earl and Jamie building the railing; Earl and Ben cutting the grass at the farm and cleaning the pond; Anne leaving cookies and date-nut bread at the front door; people sending cards with messages of love and hope; Frank and Sylvia bringing chocolate Band-Aids and aspirin along with papers from the office; so many others sending flowers and coming to visit, and calling, and sending their prayers.*

*I hesitate to put this in here, naming names again, knowing there are countless others who helped us get through this difficult time, who showed their love, showering us with their love and concern. To all of you, my family's and my undying gratitude.

June 8, 2000: This is love in a human body lying on the bed, the dark core of the rose towards which the honeybee dives seeking the elixir, this man lying naked on the hospital bed, breath coming and going, a tide of soft air, the door opening and closing, as one person after another comes in, then leaves, this focus of my world where I too stay close, not wanting to leave, all plans cancelled as he asked, to stay by his side, watching, listening, tethered by a lifetime of devotion, making amends for past unkindness, finding again what I had lost, the boundaries of what is essential, the simple truth of the goodness of life, the all there is, or needs be.

Bernie died as he had lived, with grace, kindness, and gentleness, and, to the extent that it was possible, on his own terms, given that he did not want what was happening to happen any more than we did. He taught us all—his nurses, doctors, family, friends, colleagues—how to live and how to die. He had a will of steel and the strength of a number of men, yet it was his softness that was his most outstanding quality. But you know this from having read his memoirs. It is my hope that this account of his last ordeal will inspire you, as it does me, to greater compassion.

It was an honor to know Bernie, as is shown by what people were kind enough to write and to share about him. I will simply add what comes to my mind, that after the funeral service, after the beautiful words Rabbi Katz and Earl spoke, as the almost 700 mourners were leaving Temple Sinai, a number of people said, "We have to be more like Bernie."

July 3, 2001

David, Deborah, Jane, Bernie and Rachel at Jaime's wedding (1987)

Miriam, Bernie, Jaime and Jane (1986)

To Dad

Editor's Note: This was a collaboration of thoughts by Bernie's children and read at his funeral by Rabbi Katz.

Thank you for giving us life.

Thank you for surviving the unspeakable, and for then finding your voice to tell us.

Thank you for showing how you can bear witness to horrific evil, but turn your energy into love and peace.

Thank you for showing us that family is everything.

Thank you for instilling within us a powerful spirituality.

Thank you for sharing your love of nature with us.

Thank you for loving us for who we are.

Thank you for loving our spouses like your own children and our stepchildren like our own children.

Thank you for instilling within us a love of justice and righteousness.

Thank you for teaching us to face bigotry and inhumanity with gentleness and fortitude.

Thank you for showing us true courage.

Thank you for helping us through this wrenching period.

Thank you for letting us help you.

Thank you for your most wondrous smile.

Thank you for being such a wonderful, loving, inspiring father.

Thank you for the laughter and your constant humor.

Thank you for your unending patience and your guidance.

Thank you for the kisses and hugs, over the years, and over the miles.

Thank you for giving us the chance to feel what true unconditional love is, always, and unending.

Thank you for all memories and lessons from beginning to end, that will have to sustain us from now on.

Thank you for your love.

Thank you for the beautiful songs and lullabies that you sang for us.

Thank you for being there to help when help was needed.

Thank you for so genuinely appreciating even the small gifts, kindnesses, or service that we gave to you.

Thank you for bringing wonderful people into our lives.

Thank you for the many ways in which you set a fine example, including your example of hard work, service to others, and devotion to loved ones.

Thank you for being such a lovable and endearing person.

Thank you for your parting gifts of love, which will help sustain us throughout the remainder of our lives, during which we will miss you greatly.

Early Morning Farewell to Bernie Schuster

Editor's Note: Anthony Piccione was a poet and longtime mentor to Jane. Overe the years he developed a very close relationship with Bernie

Slumped at the table, alive to the words of one who survived until yesterday, what can I offer except to weep into my hands? But a sudden music pushes out through the radio, a surprise rises in my chest, a sweeping half-memory of Persia, or Syria, Jerusalem maybe, the strong softness of women in dance, the wisp of wind, the evening hushing down its moist whisper.

What have I been welcomed into so easily? That time goes on furling around our feet in delicate surround? That what has left us keeps arriving, returned, just out of reach? I'll taste this delight, I think, for my friend so still in body, so majestically now a part of the breeze, dust, air, figs, shouts, so much the shiver of breath, shoulder, veil, so nearly always near.

Anthony Piccione
July 18, 2000

Anthony Piccione and Jane

BERNARD (BERL) SCHUSTER
May 17, 1928 – July 17, 2000

Editor's Note: This eulogy was delivered by Rabbi Alan Katz at Bernie's funeral services held at Temple Sinai in Rochester, New York. Over 700 people attended the services and hundreds went along to witness his internment at the historic Mount Hope Cemetery.

How does one begin to describe Bernie? Most of us would start out with words like kindness, generous, sweet and loving. But alone those words sound too trite to give just due to this most wonderful of human beings.

Anything we say must be put into context of where Bernie came from, what he experienced and how he then chose to live the rest of his life. If there is any one single individual who can be seen as a role model for people who have suffered and still are able to find the goodness and love in the world, it was Bernie Schuster.

Rabbi Katz and Bernie.

The tributes for Bernie are coming from all people, young and old. Jane told me a recent incident when two employees of Reynolds Arcade, where Bernie worked, came to help them rearrange his bedroom so that Bernie could spend these last few weeks at home and not in the hospital. Joshua and Philip came to the house out of the kindness of their hearts, and set up the room. They told Jane that they too loved Bernie because he never looked down on the little people. To Bernie there were no little people. As they departed they requested a copy of his book, I Will Die Tomorrow, But Not Today. Their last request was that Bernie sign the book for them. They left with this treasure in their arms.

Bernie touched and loved so many people. So many of us here today felt that true unconditional love. Bernie's way of counteracting the evil of his past was to fill the world with goodness and love. First there was family. Many of us I am sure feel that we were part of the Schuster family. That was a gift given to us. Jane and Bernie created a warm and loving home where all were made to feel welcome. Bernie was greatly appreciative of being welcomed into Jane's family and thanks his mother-in-law, Rose Moress Pressberg. These last few weeks were not easy, but Jane knows that this time together strengthened their lifelong bond. Many people were able to visit them a few weeks ago in celebration of their 45 years together.

Bernie loved his children and grandchildren with all his heart. With each of you he had his special relationship. Deborah and David, Jamie and Jessica and Miriam. May each of you take from the goodness of your father and cherish it by ensuring that it is part and parcel of all that you do. You each offered your love and support these last months as he had given to you throughout the years.

Anyone who knew Bernie also knew how important his grandchildren were to him. Rachel, Christina, Laura, Sarah and Saul, each of you were a special precious gift to your grandfather. You brought joy and light to him and after the tragic loss of so many family members in Europe, you were his way of seeing good triumph over the evil. He wrote his book for you. But also he set a living model before your eyes, minds and hearts of how a person can live a kind and loving life.

Bernie was not just a parent, grandparent and role model for his own immediate family. Whether it is in his book, or in reflections people have shared or just in casual conversations, so many, too many to name, were and continue to be seen as Bernie's children and grandchildren. If you have been told this or have felt it then you have received a blessing. Just the other day Mollie Friedman wrote a beautiful letter to Bernie. Here are some of her words, which speak for many others.

> "...I want you to know you are a role model and a person I admire. You live life to the fullest and find the best in others...most of all you're a good friend and great person...
>
> I see the full moon glowing with light. This moon reminds me of you, a very strong person glowing with pride, nothing more excellent...Bernie, I love you and I don't know one person who doesn't...
>
> This note is to let you know what a great person, an admirable person, you are, as a Jew, a lawyer and a friend."

Bernie's background can be found in his book. After losing most of his family, he finally came to Rochester to live with his aunt and uncle. But rather than work in their meat business, he chose to get an education on his own. He learned English quickly enough to get a high school degree in just one year. He was always grateful for the assistance of Carlos DeZafra. He then went on to University of Rochester and Harvard Law.

We are aware of what a fine attorney Bernie was. He viewed the law as a helping profession. He saw to it that he used his profession to assist others through the complexities of life. Bernie was always excluded from the subject when lawyer jokes were told. He brought goodness and caring into the legal profession. Justice was important to him. He would listen to the wisdom of his heart to always do the right thing.

Bernie loved nature and his farm. A place where he planted thousands of trees. A recent planting was a weeping cherry for his deceased brother Maische, who loved cherries. Bernie's loving nature was not only felt by people, but also by animals. Many of the wildlife would approach him without fear.

Jane asked me to share the poem "The Peace of Wild Things" by Wendell Berry.

When despair for the world grows in me
And I wake in the night at the least sound
In fear of what my life and my children's lives may be,
I go and lie down where the wood drake
Rests in his beauty on the water, and the great heron feeds.
I come into the peace of wild things
Who do not tax their lives with forethought of grief.
I come into the presence of still water.
And I feel above me the day-blind stars
Waiting with their light. For a time
I rest in the grace of the world, and am free.

One truly gets an insight into how Bernie's love of nature connected to his outlook of life. His farm was his place of peace and serenity. He loved to plant, work the land and even if the tractor was driven into the pond and had to be rescued by Harley. This was his joy.

As a survivor of the Holocaust, Bernie was initially unable to speak of his experiences. But when he became able to share, he would speak all over. He spoke at Roberts Wesleyan, at the Uof R and at Brockport, to name a few institutions of higher learning. He co-chaired the Auschwitz Exhibit at MCC and served as chair of the Holocaust Commission at the Federation. I am sure to be leaving out many other places where Bernie's presence and words helped to teach and keep memory alive.

He used his words and life as a rebuttal to what he witnessed. He counteracted the horrors and brutality with tremendous positive energy. He used goodness, generosity of spirit and resources and love to combat the darkness.

Even during his last weeks of suffering Bernie had smiles for those who visited him. He was truly pleased to see people when he was able. While in tremendous pain he remained ever kind and thoughtful. Jamie told me of his last visit to the hospital when they requested an ambulance crew with strong men to carry him through the tight corners of his home. After a crew of two women bumped him around, even scraping his arm and totally exhausting him finally left him off at home, he reminded Jamie to thank them and give them a big tip for their services.

In Bernie's memories he cites a favorite song, This world is a narrow bridge and the main thing is not to be afraid. In Hebrew we sing *Kol Haolam Kulo, Gesher Tzar Me'od, V'haiker lo l'fachaid klal.* The Yiddish Bernie knew, (which I beg your pardon as to pronunciation is) *Olam aze is a shmoler brik un deriker is nisht zum shrerekn zich.*

As we remember Bernie and learn from his life, we should act with the love and kindness he always exhibited. The world may be a narrow bridge, but if we live as he did it will be a place in which all of us can feel secure from the spirit of love that we felt from Bernie Schuster.

EULOGY FOR BERNIE

Editor's Note: Bernie stipulated that his funeral not be a morbid affair. As such, he wanted only one person to deliver his eulogy, his longtime friend Earl Wensel.

To spend only a few minutes speaking about a man so important to my life is going to be difficult for me. I could talk about him endlessly, although I would much prefer to listen to him talk, as I always learned so much from him.

It is easy for me to say of Bernie:

He was courageous (we all know what we went through as a child).
He was full of kindness and giving.
He was sensitive to everyone's needs.
He was a wonderful storyteller – we have all listened to him tell us about the past.
He was successful in his business, at the law, in his marriage.

But, when I really think about talking about Bernie, I come to this – FAMILY.

The key to Bernie Schuster's life was and will continue to be – family.

If you knew Bernie you were a part of his family... you could not avoid it. Why? That's easy, too. As easy as reading from the dedication to his book. Bernie wrote:

.... to my parents, brother and sisters
who did not survive the Holocaust
and whose love and nurturing
gave me the strength to survive...

Ginny and Earl Wenzel

Bernie was always part of a large family. In Jasinowka, his home in Poland, he was the youngest of an immediate family of ten, but he always said, he was sure he was related to pretty much everyone in the town. The horror that was the Holocaust brutally took most of that wonderful family. Bernie survived and came to America, and I truly believe, set forth in his life to rebuild, maintain and keep safe, all of his remaining family and family values.

Over the years, Bernie and Jane have raised three wonderful children of their own: Deborah, Jamie, and Miriam. And, the family has grown with five beautiful grandchildren: Christie, Laura, Rachel Ann, Sarah Elizabeth, and Saul Benjamin. As you are well aware, these grandchildren have been the greatest pride of Bernie's life. And, I have to say, he and Jane practiced grandparenting with our sons, Andy and Ben. Because Ginny's parents and mine were too far away to be available on Grandparents Day at school, Bernie and Jane were adopted as grandparents on more then one occasion. The boys loved it and I think Bernie and Jane did, too.

Bernie's family has been local and it has been international, worldwide. When he could he would visit cousins in New York and New Jersey; Jane's brother and family in North Carolina or California; cousins and nieces and nephews in Canada. And, there were trips to Mexico to visit his sister Feitche and her husband Shleime in Mexico; cousins in Israel, and his brother Maishe and his family in Australia. He wanted to spend as much time as he could always with all the members of his family.

Bernie loved music. He loved to sing Yiddish songs to the children. He enjoyed attending RPO concerts. And, the recitals. I am sure he never missed a recital that any of the children played. Like all of us, Bernie had favorite music and songs. Bernie wrote of one of them in his book. He wrote about the students from a Yeshiva coming to spend several weeks in Jasionowka before Passover, while their school was being prepared for the holidays. The students would stay with the villagers and Bernie remembered going to the synagogue and singing with them. Even as an adult, he would recall and sing the words of a song of that time in his life:

Olam Aze	This World
Is a Shmoler Brik	Is a Narrow Bridge
Un Deriker, Un Deriker	And the Main Thing, And the Main Thing
Is Nisht Zum Shrerekn Zich	Is Not to be Afraid

Saturday mornings with Bernie were special. It meant THE FARM. But, before the farm, there was the CharBroil on Monroe Avenue for coffee and breakfast. Bernie would always say, "Wensel, are you going to have coffee?" That was the tease...I never drank coffee. Usually, it would be Bernie, me, Jamie and Saul. But, everyone was welcome.

The CharBroil was another extension of the family. Everywhere one looked there was family: John Parinello and his sons and grandchildren, the TV-10 newsman and his new daughter (We watched when he first carried her in as a newborn in her small carrier and then we all smiled at her first steps earlier this year. There was Becky the waitress and the stories about her son. There were the law school buddies; the people from the downtown Four Corners, all the people from Temple. There was Saul Benjamin building castles from coffee creams and jam singles.

The CharBroil was about family too. Saul would say, in amazement, "Grandpa, do you know everyone here?" Bernie would respond, "Yes, I do!"

Then we were off to The Farm.

We always tried to think up a better name. But, we always came back to—The Farm—56 acres of paradise for Bernie's family. We didn't farm in the agrarian sense, but all wonder of things were grown in the family-sense.

Bernie cherished trees. In over thirty years, we (Bernie, me, our sons, his grandchildren and many others) planted trees of all kinds at the farm, and it was and is our responsibility to care for them as Bernie has.

Bernie designed and had dug a pond. So there would be the peace that sitting beside the water provides. He put up a beautiful swing that seats four, so a group could enjoy it together. He stocked the pond with bass, and trout, and carp. The fish could be caught, but they were always put back. I've made friends with many of them—they follow me around the pond.

Bernie cut firewood for the family fireplaces. He built many trails so we could all enjoy the ease of walking through the quiet woods of the Farm.

And, Bernie fought the geese. Oh, did he fight the geese. Usually, the geese won.

We watched Bernie change the farm from just fields and a swamp, to a place with all the comforts of home (at first, just sheds and an outhouse, Jane's palace, he called it.) Today, besides all of the trees, berry patch, pond and trails, it includes a wonderful home that, amazingly, we all tried to talk him out of building – at least where he built it.

Bernie wanted to put the house at the bottom of a hill that literally drained into the pond. We thought, this will be a disaster. We were sure it would flood away.

Today, that house is built exactly where Bernie wanted it and it has the driest basement of any house I know. The house and the farm are a haven, a respite from the busy life of the city. Bernie so loved to be there and loved it even more when his family was there with him.

Let me turn again to Bernie's book one more time. Bernie wrote:

What has my life, with all its trials and tribulations, taught me? What, if anything, can I pass on to you, my dearest grandchildren? Having survived the Holocaust years, I was determined to do whatever I could to help make this world a better place. I have not been in a position to help do away with man's inhumanity to man.

Wars continue to plague us. Hatred and strife have lifted their ugly head again and again. We are as yet not turning or swords into plowshares and have yet to come to love our neighbors as ourselves. Still, I feel that you, my grandchildren, will continue to make progress toward making this world a better place for you and generations to follow. I hope you will never stop trying to do so.

Individually, I have tried to help as many people as I could. I have tried to listen to people and to give of my time and energies so that their pain, fears and troubles might be diminished.

Have I achieved all that I might have? Not likely. Have attempts been wasted? Not at all Bessie Anderson Stanley set forth what she considered a successful life. She writes:

"He has achieved success
who has lived well,
laughed often and loved much;
who has enjoyed
the respect of intelligent men
and the love of children;
who has filled his niche
and accomplished his task;
who has left the world better
than he found it...
who never lacked appreciation
of earth's beauty
or failed to express it;
who has always looked for
the best in others
and gave them the best he had..."

It is my hope that you, my loved ones, will feel that my life has been truly successful. It is my further hope that you will strive to set such goals for yourselves that will allow you to succeed. I hope that you will love yourselves and the people near and dear to you; that you will help others and make the world a better place for all living beings. We live in a beautiful world, and each of us has an opportunity and the responsibility to conduct our lives in such a way as to enhance its beauty.

Bernie,

You have reached out to countless souls with boundless compassion. You have told your story that we might know you, understand and truly touch history. You have planted and built and made the face of nature even more glorious.

Now, having known you and having been included in your family, we are obligated to reach out as you have, to care and nurture as you have; to love and live to joy as you have, and to spread the limitless goodness that you have left with us.

Life with you was worth every cup of coffee I never drank – and so much, much more.

BE WITH GOD MY DEAR FRIEND.

The beauty and solitude of his Victor Farm was a favorite getaway for Bernie & the family

1975

זִכְרוֹנוֹ לִבְרָכָה.

Zich-ro-no-li-v'ra-cha.

His memory is a blessing.

1995

ZOG NIT KEINMOL (SONG OF THE PARTISANS)

Words by Hirsch Glik*

Zog nit keinmol
az du geist
dem letzten veg
farshteln bloie teg.
Val kumen
vet noch unzer
oisgebenkte sho
S'vet a poik ton
unzer trot
Mir gainen do

You must not say that you now walk the final way,
because the darkened heavens hide the blue of day.
The time we've longed for will at last draw near,
and our steps, as drums, will sound that we are here.

Fun grinem palmen-land
biz vaisen land fun shnay
mir zainin dau
mit unzer paiyin
mit unzer vay
un vu gealin s'iz.
Ah shpritz fun unzer blut
vet ah shprotz ton unzer gevurah
unzer mut.

From land all green with palms, to lands all white with snow,
we now arrive with all our pain and all our woe.
Where our blood sprayed out and came to touch the land,
There our courage and our faith will rise and stand.

*Of all the songs of all the ghettos, the one that spread like wildfire was the Song of the Partisans by Hirsh Glik. It used a tune by the Soviet brothers Pokras, and became the official resistance hymn of all the Eastern European partisan brigades. It was translated into Hebrew, Polish, Russian, Spanish, Romanian, Dutch, and English. It was well known in all the concentration camps. Hirsh Glik was born in 1920 in Vilna.When the ghetto was liquidated, he was sent to a concentration camp in Estonia. He escaped from the camp and joined the partisans, and died while fighting as a partisan.

Diary of a Survivor

BIALYSTOK 1939-1945

Yiddish manuscript written by Feitche Schuster

Translated into English by Max Rosenfeld

Dedicated to my dear parents,

Yaakov and Haya-Soreh Schuster,

my sisters, my brother, their children,

our entire family,

who perished . . .

The town of Jasionowka, located in the Bialystok Region of Poland about forty kilometers from the big city of Bialystok, was so small it was not even marked on the map. Of its two thousand inhabitants, fifteen hundred were Jews. Life was peaceful there. The marketplace stood quietly in the cen ter of town with its church and a few Jewish shops. There were no special market days, no regular fairs. The people earned their living by hard, honest toil in this town known for its tanneries; one of them was famous throughout the country—the Skurdamik company which belonged to the Minski family. A supplier of leather for the Polish military, it was renowned for its high quality product. In addition, there were a number of smaller tanneries which worked for the private market and employed hundreds of people.

Jasionowka was really far ahead of the surrounding towns in its productivity. The hide-scraps were used in other enterprises, such as glue factories, and there were shops for washing the animal-hair. Naturally, there was a Tanners Union, with its own long history. The Jewish and Polish workers lived together peacefully, with the same troubles and the same joys. Life proceeded normally. Every morning the factory whistles called Jews and Poles to their jobs. Together they celebrated the First of May. Together they went on strike. And together they rejoiced when the strike ended in victory.

Since early spring we have been hearing rumors of war. A feeling of apprehension touches everyone, but soon passes. The dark clouds evaporate. The sky clears up. The summer goes by and we forget all the ugly talk.

But one fine September morning we are jolted out of our slumber. MOBILIZATION! Now it becomes clear. The Deitsch has invaded Poland's borders. A "holiday" in our town—no one goes to work. But no one stays at home, either. The men run to get their mobilization cards. Women and children stand around aimlessly in the streets. The news flies from mouth to mouth—all able-bodied men will soon be conscripted. Women weep. A babel of shouts, cries, rumors.

Two large trucks pull up. All the men who have been ordered to report for duty stand ready. It takes only a few minutes. Quick farewells. The men clamber up into the trucks. The trucks roar and speed away. The crowd gradually thins out. But no one can rest easily. Everybody's thoughts are ominous—the Germans are so strong. Their arrival will be our downfall. Hitler has threatened to "get even" with the Jews.

In the meantime, small groups of dispirited Polish soldiers march through the town. The Germans are moving ahead quickly. The news is more and more frightening. The days are difficult. The Polish government issues a decree: All able-bodied men must leave the town and report for duty. The young men are mobilized (those not in the army) and taken to Bialystok. The days and nights grow interminable.

The Deitsch is very close now. People say that as soon as the Germans enter a town or village they shoot up the streets. We grow tense with waiting. A peasant comes running with the news that the German army has already taken a village a few kilometers away. Jews and non-Jews alike are filled with the same anxiety. The streets are deserted. A deathly silence engulfs the town. The first reconnaissance motorcycles ride into town. No one is in the streets to meet them. Everything goes smoothly, uneventfully. This is not at all what we have been led to expect from Nazi Germans, except for the report that a kilometer away, on the road, they shot a Polish student for no apparent reason.

With us, however, they are not behaving badly, only that they move into all the bigger homes for several days and "buy" the last bit of goods in Jewish stores—goods worth hundreds of *zloty*—for a few German marks. If anyone dares to complain, they reply that very soon the Soviet Russians will be here and will simply confiscate everything without paying a penny. This news spreads through the town like wildfire. Jews dance for joy. Anybody will be better than the Hitlerites. But perhaps the joy is premature? Yet during the night the Germans pack up and drive off, leaving the way open for the Red Army. Oh happy Jewish town! Excitement! Jubilation! We wait impatiently for the Red Army. What will it look like?

Meanwhile Jasionowka has no government, no authorities, which makes people a little uneasy. But soon things will be happier.

Truly joyous, with singing and cheering, is the mood when the first Soviet tanks roll in. For us, this army is something new. They stop in the marketplace, call people over, chat with them. They seem eager to talk with us. And we with them. What has happened to yesterday's fear? The entire town surrounds them. Children climb up on the tanks. People who yesterday were so frightened, afraid to show their faces in the windows, are now riding all over town with the Red Army soldiers like heroes. The working people come to life, bold, proud—certain that the Red Army is offering them a friendly, comradely hand; they will all work together for the good of the great Soviet Union.

A new life begins, with new forms. Gradually we grow accustomed to it. We become Soviet. Even stronger grows our satisfaction with the Soviets when, a few at a time, Jews begin coming to our town from the German-occupied sections of Poland. We are all happy. Now we and our families can feel at home. Jews have equal rights, equal citizenship. The refugees tell us that in Germany, Jews are simply disappearing—they are picked up on the street and no one knows what happens to them. They tell us that all the Jews in Germany will be sent to concentration camps.

Most of the people who come to our town are men who have been separated from their families and are roaming the countryside, trying to stay alive. The women have been allowed to stay where they were. In the meantime, all the Jews are being forced into crowded ghettos.

So here in Jasionowka we feel lucky. (A town with a working-class population, it was therefore privileged.) Life is not going badly. Everyone is employed. Jews and non-Jews live together harmoniously. Whatever signs of anti-Semitism there had been have now vanished completely, as though we had entered the long-promised era when people will not even remember that such evils ever existed in the world.

But soon we hear rumors of war again. Although Germany and the Soviet Union are now "friends," we feel certain that that situation will not last very long. The intellectuals, however, say that for the Germans to attack the Soviets now would be suicidal, and therefore war between them is impossible. It is much more pleasant to think this way. People can sleep peacefully again. Why worry, when the mighty Red Army is watching over us?

If the world's leading statesmen did not foresee the naked aggression of the Germans, how could ordinary people have expected that on one fine June morning, the 22nd, Germany would suddenly invade the Soviet Union? A Sunday morning after a happy Saturday evening. The people of our town, yesterday so content, are now hopeless and despairing. The first ones to go and join the Red Army are the Soviet citizens who have come from the east. All the work places are mobilized. It all happens so unexpectedly that no one knows what to do. One can sense that something is not in order. The Russian kommissar in our town tries to put people at ease, assuring them that the enemy is being repulsed. But that same evening he himself prepares to leave. The chaos becomes intolerable. People are terror-stricken. Everyone tries to read in the faces of others what they should do to escape. We are sure of only one thing—the Germans will spare no Jew here, especially Soviet Jews. And with each passing hour the urge to live grows stronger. For us, the Deitsch means death. People who are close to the government apparatus, who work in responsible positions, feel the danger even more keenly.

We are sure of only one thing — the Germans will spare no Jew here, especially Soviet Jews. And with each passing hour the urge to live grows stronger. For us, the Deitsch means death.

The town is sunk in gloom. From time to time, tattered remnants of the Soviet armed forces pass through the area. Some of them try to allay our fears: the Germans will never reach our town, they will be driven back before they ever get here. But the disorder of the Red Army is demoralizing. They seem to have fallen apart. They themselves are at a loss which way to go. One thing everyone agrees on—there must have been a betrayal by certain Soviet leaders.

But that knowledge doesn't help our situation here. Quite the contrary. Everyone knows a horrible time is near. More than one of us will die. (It never occurred to us that almost everyone would die.) The mood is oppressive. Faces darken. From day to day, things grow worse. The German army is advancing relentlessly. Occasionally an isolated Soviet automobile drives by, but actually, where can it go, when their army is encircled?

The general morale in Jasionowka sinks lower and lower. Soon the most corrupt elements among the Poles sense the defenselessness of the Jews. They don't even wait for the Germans to arrive.

They are already coming in from the villages, breaking into Jewish homes, looting in broad daylight, destroying whatever they cannot carry away with them. (They felt at once that they now had powerful support: the Germans would not stop them, would in fact encourage them. This was done, of course, by individuals with the basest instincts. The Polish workers in our town tried to stop them. The priest Lozowski put up strong resistance, called upon the people to oppose such criminal behavior. But the intoxication of looting was irresistible.)

Several days pass this way. The Jews themselves are now waiting impatiently for the Germans, for they will certainly put a stop to such violence. Although the approach of the German army is frightening, the present situation is worse. People cannot live this way for long. Our vulnerability is obvious, but we can do nothing. The Jews who left with the Red Army are no better off. Some return, having nowhere else to go. Where could one flee on foot, or even in a car, when the Germans are moving forward on all fronts, with planes and tanks, destroying everything along the way?

On the highways lie wrecked vehicles, battered corpses. No matter how resolute or how energetic you are, the only thing you can do is resign yourself to a situation with no way out. During the first days people still tried to create illusions. Now it is clear to all: today or tomorrow the German murderers will be in our town. It is inevitable.

The days are hot, uneasy. People are listless, weary. They stare silently at the highway. The town seems muffled, like the air before a storm. The week drags on endlessly. It is difficult to find a place for yourself. Whatever is going to happen, let it happen more quickly. Nerves are at the breaking point.

Now! A roaring of motors. German planes fly low, circling the town. Slowly, arrogantly, the German soldiers ride in. Polish women, bunches of flowers in their hands, come out to greet the conquerors, happy to see their guests who are going to lighten all their burdens. The Germans are very friendly, accept the flowers graciously. They want to know if there are Jews in Jasionowka and how they have behaved toward the Poles. At once some unscrupulous peasants appear with complaints about what Jews did to them. The Germans are more than willing to listen. They promise the peasants a bit of fun with the Jews.

The panic among the Jews mounts from moment to moment. What will happen next? Is it really possible that the Germans will not let us live? How can they murder a whole town full of Jews? No, it can never happen!

This is routine practice for them whenever they occupy a town or city in which there are Jews.

It doesn't take long and they are breaking windows in our synagogues. One sees Jews running through the streets, their heads bloody. The panic among the Jews mounts from moment to moment. What will happen next? Is it really possible that the Germans will not let us live? How can they murder a whole town full of Jews? No, it can never happen!

The same thought is in everyone's head: the only way to escape death is to run away during the first twenty-four hours, because the rumor is that the German army is permitted—encouraged—to kill Jews when it first marches into a place.

First come the Storm Troopers, ready to do whatever they please. Then come many soldiers—young, strong, arrogant. World conquerors, members of a superior race, they look down on everyone from a great height.

But to us, Deitsch means Evil, Terror, Death. None of us had understood this before. Poor little Jewish town! What has happened to your charm? What do they want of us, these parasites who have taken unto themselves the right to decide whether Jews live or die? Doesn't even one of them stop to think of what they are about to do? Will they all go unpunished? Where is their conscience? Their culture? Is this the twentieth century? Are they not ashamed to commit such atrocities upon defenseless men, women, babies? Is there no one among them to condemn this? They are all drunk with their easy victory. No one bars their way. The helpless get out of their path, try to hide from their eyes.

Accursed Friday evening. Every Jewish family tries to get away from its home. As one has legs, one must run. But where can they run to? No one offers a helping hand. Jews peer out of curtained windows and watch the Poles moving about freely in the streets. They are not afraid of the Germans; they walk alongside them, make friends with them, try to help them. And there are many ways to be helpful—pointing out where Jews live, which Jew is wealthy, which Jew is a worker, which Jew is a Communist. By so doing, they seal the fate of many people.

A sleepless night. No one is concerned now about abandoning the home which he has worked so hard for, in a community which generations have toiled to establish. People leave their dwellings, run out into the fields, hide among the cornstalks, hoping the Germans won't find them. It is terrible to watch the innocent children who cannot understand why they are being punished this way. People climb up into attics, cower in cellars. Nowhere does it feel safe enough. They keep searching for better hiding places. They try to interpret the noises in the street. The Germans are busy getting themselves settled.

The darkness comes as a sort of consolation, a respite. The German soldiers are still afraid to go searching in the dark corners for their victims. Why should they? They know that sooner or later they will get their hands on everyone. No one will be able to hide forever....

Summer. The June night is short. The day arrives fearfully. Early morning. Frightened faces peer out of doorways. A few "scouts" go out to learn what has happened during the night. Quiet. No news. Only the soldiers start moving around. For them, a workday is beginning.

Soon the military is fully awake. First they carry out of the synagogue the Torah scrolls that Jews have not managed to hide. With their helpers from the town they pour gasoline over the scrolls and set fire to them. Laughing in glee, they stand around watching the Torah scrolls burn.

Finished with the synagogue, they turn their attention to the Jewish homes, break open doors, invite the Poles to take whatever they please. But the most valuable things the Germans take for themselves. Their helpers grab whatever is left. A joyous time is beginning for them. And why not? They can see that the Germans are right—Jews have all the wealth, which they will now "inherit" quickly and easily. Their only regret is that they cannot take everything their eyes see; they can't decide what to take first. Peasants who live closer to Jasionowka drive their wagons into town. Those who live farther store the stolen goods in places close to town and go back for more. It's too good an opportunity to let pass. They can pile up enough things now to last a lifetime.

Never before has Jasionowka seen such a holiday. For the non-Jews it's a real carnival. The Jews sit in their hiding places and watch the looting with growing anxiety. They can think about only one thing—will their lives be taken, too? By comparison, all their stolen property is a trivial thing.

Lozowski the priest is extremely upset by all this. Whenever there are no Germans around he tries to stop the looting—even using his stick when words don't help. He threatens the looters with the worst punishments of hell for committing such terrible sins. But the temptation is too great. So much valuable property—which they could never hope to acquire even by years of hard work—is practically begging to be taken. And the people in this town are not lazy—they cart off loads of bedding, clothing, overcoats, fur coats, furniture, sewing machines, bicycles, clocks, dishes. Never has there been such a fair! Whatever they see, they need. Nothing in the world can stop them.

And the SS men in their smart, brown uniforms, overjoyed with their great success, keep looking for new sources of entertainment. Where are all the Jews hiding while their homes are being ransacked? The Germans and their local helpers run all through the town searching in cellars and attics.

They drive out a group of Jews whose terror-stricken eyes plead: What do you want of us? What will you do to us? Haven't you already done enough?

But the Germans and their helpers are having a wonderful time—they won't let even one Jew get away! They take their victims to the house of Abraham Rosenblum and throw them all into the cellar like sacks of potatoes. Young toughs, experienced in their "work," are enjoying every minute of it. And the Germans run around bellowing like enraged bulls as they round up more and more Jews for the cellar. Then they place a heavy rock over the entrance.

Inside the cellar it is terribly crowded. Some of the people are having trouble breathing. Their groaning only makes things worse in the darkness. Perhaps these are their last moments on earth. For a few of the Jews there it was.

After a while a German soldier enters the cellar and orders everyone to surrender their money, jewelry and other valuables. The Jews feel a little better. If that's all the German wants. Whatever they are carrying of value they give to the German, who gladly accepts everything, adding only that he intends to search everyone there. Having collected everything, he fires his automatic several times into the crowd, climbs out of the cellar and replaces the rock over the entrance. Below, there is panic. Hysteria. Weeping. Groans of the dying.

Feitche and Shleime Schuster in Giadalajara, Mexico.

Feitche and Jane at our wedding. (1955)

Shleime, Jane, Berl and Feitche on our wedding day. (1955)

As soon as the Germans leave, a woman who had been hiding nearby runs out and pushes the rock away. The Jews come out of their tomb and count their dead: five. Eliyohu Chaim Treshchanski and his two daughters, fourteen and fifteen years old. Also, Chatzkl Ostroburski and a stranger who had escaped from his town. In despair, Treshchanski's widow climbs out of the cellar and runs to the German headquarters, screaming: "You have killed my husband and my children! Shoot me, too! I don't want to live without them!"

The German looks at her and smiles. "We only shoot those who want to live. You can live and suffer a little longer. When we're good and ready, we'll shoot you. Not before."

The news spreads to other streets. People start fleeing from the town but it doesn't take long for the Germans to put a stop to this. They round up Jews and line them up against the wall of the church. People try to hide. But the Germans set fire to houses on several streets. The marketplace goes up in flames. The SS men run out into the cornfields, searching; the non-Jews help them, carrying big clubs. Anyone who resists, they beat to death, as they did to Moyshe Bernard. They drag his family over to the church, threatening to kill them all.

The heat is oppressive.
The fire and smoke
from the neighboring
streets is suffocating.
People faint,
but no one brings them
any water.
Children fall unconscious.
For several hours
the Jews stand there
in anguish,
awaiting death.

Now they have rounded up almost all the Jews in Jasionowka. Whoever cannot walk, they shoot on the spot—Hershl Rosenblatt, 75 years old, a wonderful, friendly man, and Mula Starovolski, who happened to be sick at the time. Meir Jonah Zimmer and his wife are killed by some peasants. First they beat them and break their arms, then they throw them alive into the fire. Kubik, a peasant from a nearby village, stabs Shifra Azev to death. The Germans shoot Kasriel Fadlipski as he is praying in his *tallis* and *tefillin* and throw him into the fire. The next morning we find seventy corpses.

The rest of the Jews are forced to stand for a long time outside the church, watching their *shtetl* burn down. The Germans face them with machine-guns. The non-Jews are armed with clubs. The Jews now realize they will all die here, but by what means they don't know.

Meanwhile, trucks keep riding by, carrying German troops. Some stop and ask what's going on. The answer they get is that the Jews set fire to the town.

Some mothers approach the Germans and implore them to let the children live, at least. They weep, fall on their knees, beg for a bit of water for their children. The Germans are busy taking pictures. Kaluska, a peasant who has been helping the Germans, suggests that while they are waiting, they shoot a hundred Jews. The German refuses; he doesn't have orders to do that. When the time comes, he will shoot them all. Meanwhile he must wait. Kaluska pleads for permission to shoot at least ten—he will do it himself. But the German insists: orders are orders. The peasants curse the Jews in the foulest language. None of them shows any feelings of pity.

The heat is oppressive. The fire and smoke from the neighboring streets is suffocating. People faint, but no one brings them any water. Children fall unconscious. For several hours the Jews stand there in anguish, awaiting death. Nearby, on the street, lies the body of a little Jewish girl. No one knows whose child she is. Apparently she belongs to no one from Jasionowka. No one moves the body. The Jews are certain that soon they will all be lying on the street like that. The only question is whether the Germans will shoot them, beat them to death or burn them alive. Mothers, looking at their suffering children, cannot restrain their tears. Some begin to pray for the end to come more quickly.

A car drives up. Inside sits a German officer, bringing new orders. The organizers of this evil game run up to him. The officer wants to know why the Jews should die in such an easy, painless way. Let them live a while longer—we can always finish them off. To the Jews he says:

"You yourselves set fire to your own homes—remember that! This time we'll spare you. The next time you do something like this you'll all be beaten to death! Now go back to your homes!"

But where can they go? Some of them no longer have homes. Those whose houses are still standing find nothing left but four walls. No beds, no bedding, not even a plate to eat from, even if there had been any food. But there is nothing to eat. And what about those who ran into the fields and villages? Some of them had been lucky enough to find a farmer who had let them stay overnight in a barn. Many of them had to stay out in the open, watching the Germans torment the Jews.

A gang of young toughs goes searching through the fields and villages, wherever they suspect Jews to be hiding. God help those who fall into their hands. They beat Yankl Schuster unconscious and bring him into town a bloody pulp. They round up a group of women and children and lead them out to be shot, but the Germans stop them before they can carry out the execution.

That Sabbath-day will remain forever in the memories of the few of us who survived. Toward evening the air turned cooler and rain poured down as if heaven itself were weeping over the Jewish fate. Everyone was exhausted. There was not the least bit of comfort anywhere. In the morning, despite their fear of venturing outdoors, they began gathering up the dead. A few of the older men took care of the burials. The young men who survived were afraid to appear in the street.

In the meantime, the Germans have begun to restore order. Several Poles volunteer to help them. They form a militia. Leon Kovnacki is appointed town commandant and serves the Hitlerites very devotedly. Gradski, the schoolteacher, conducts a search of Jewish homes, looking for hidden weapons. In the process he behaves very cruelly, although he himself, when he was arrested in 1939 by the Soviet authorities, was freed thanks to a Jewish petition. But he has forgotten all that. He and his helpers start torturing Jews, draw up a list of Jewish names and begin squeezing everyone dry.

Later that week they organize a second inquisition. The sixth of July. They are rounding up Jews again. Where will they take them? What will they do with them? They drive all the Jews into a big stable in the center of the marketplace. Once it had been the headquarters of the firefighters. Some Jews manage to hide for a while, but most of them are caught and brought to the stable. (The Gilik brothers took a great part in this action; also Edward Zibilsk and others.) As they drag their captives to the stable they beat them unmercifully. This has now become commonplace.

Meanwhile they request permission from the Gestapo to burn down the stable, along with the Jews inside. The building is ready, all doused with benzene, because they are certain that permission will be granted. In the morning a representative of the Gestapo arrives, but does not give them permission. The only orders he has is to arrest a few Jews. As usual, he starts asking for names. Someone mentions Israel Balakin (who is over seventy) because he was a deputy in the regional Soviet. (He was a deputy not because he was a Communist but because of his seniority in the tannery.) The rest of the Jews are sent home. Israel Balakin is taken to the outskirts of town—and shot.

The Polish police, seeing how defeated the Jews are, believe that now is the proper time to do what they have been wanting to do for a long time. No one will protect the Jews now.

The Polish police, seeing how defeated the Jews are, believe that now is the proper time to do what they have been wanting to do for a long time. No one will protect the Jews now. Gradski starts taking advantage of the situation. A Pole who had worked for the government before the Soviets came in, he spoke only Russian with them. Now he is a loyal German agent, does all the vilest things, blackmails Jews, arrests whomever he pleases, then releases his victims whenever he chooses. His very name strikes terror among the Jewish population.

He stops Germans who are only passing through the town and practically drags them to the homes of well-to-do Jews in order to obtain a "gift" from them. Our people no longer get any rest. Some Jews even bring Gradski gifts on their own accord, just to keep him quiet.

A few days go by "uneventfully," with only an occasional search. Then there is a fresh problem. The police come with a list and order certain Jews out of their homes. They want forty-two people—the youngest and strongest. And if any of them fail to appear, the Germans will start shooting. It is an extremely difficult decision to make. But there is no way out of this. If your name is on the list and you do not go out into the street, they will punish the whole town. In addition, the police have assured everyone that all they want to do is speak to those forty-two people and then they can return to their homes.

In any case, all forty-two report to the police. But it is the Gestapo who is waiting for them in the street. The men are ordered to line up in fours. They are marched out to work somewhere for a few days. Everybody is uneasy. There is hardly a family that isn't personally involved now. On this hot July day, without so much as a drink of water, the forty-two men are taken away, supposedly to Bialystok.

Four days pass and not one of them has returned. No one knows where they are or what has happened to them until several of them manage to escape. Then it is no longer a secret. First the Germans starved them. Then they gave them something very salty to eat. Then they refused to give them water. Then they beat them. They beat Avrom Yitzhok Ganiantski so badly around the head that he begged the other Jews to kill him. Eventually he went out of his mind and died. The Germans kept inventing new torments. They cut out Moyshe Kanya's tongue. The things they tell us are too horrible to think about. For the person with a strong constitution it was worse — he suffered more torture before death freed him. And all the others had to watch as the Germans called a few of them out for "work" every day. And although they were under heavy guard, they managed to learn that the Germans beat their victims and then shot them. Then they started shooting their victims openly, in plain sight of the others.

The few who succeeded in escaping did so when they were taken down to the river to fetch water. When their guard left them alone for a moment, they plunged into the river, swam across and hid in a forest. Eventually they made their way back to Jasionowka. For a while they stayed hidden. (They reported also that Moyshe Kaminska and Choneh Fayvl Mahler had been tortured to death.)

From day to day our situation worsens. There is no way to escape. The town is small; everyone knows everyone else. Besides, we all have non-Jewish neighbors from whom it is impossible to hide. Everyone knows that when a car drives into town and stops at Kovnacki's house there will soon be bad news. It is only a question of whose turn it is. The only way to avoid death is to make yourself invisible. Most people start staying away from their homes, sleeping in the fields.

The 18th of July. The Gestapo appears and with the help of the Polish police scours the town in a search for able-bodied men for "two hours work." Gradski notices Joshua Sidranski hiding in his garden. He runs in and drags him out. They also catch Yitzhok Dombrowski and Abraham Silberstein (he had been a schoolteacher before the Soviet days). Also, Shay Ostroburski and his son Motl; Joseph Baron, a boy of 16; Itske Azrikan, Stein, Leyb Andurski and Motya-Itche Sapoznik. All of them are taken to the police station, where they are forced to stand facing a wall. They are beaten over the head with rubber hoses until they can barely stand up. Then two cars come and take them away.

The next day some non-Jews tell us that a few kilometers from the town three men were shot in the woods. Although this is no longer news to us, we still find it hard to believe. Soon we know it for a fact. The Germans even give the families permission to take the bodies to the cemetery for burial.

First the Germans starve them. Then they give them something very salty to eat. They refuse to give them water. Then they beat them.

Whenever a car drives into town and stops, the Jews start running, mostly the men, because up until then they had not taken women in their roundups. Many of the Jews in Jasionowka live in larger homes, so they have been able to prepare hiding places. This becomes the most important thing in our lives.

Gradski does not allow us even a day's respite. If no Germans come into town he walks around with a list that he prepared himself, tells people he is empowered to arrest anyone on the list. This, of course, is an invitation for people to bribe him into not carrying out his threat.

The worst day of the week turns out to be Saturday. Not one Sabbath during this period passes peacefully. It hasn't been more than a few weeks that the Germans have been here, yet it already seems like an eternity. And we know we will never be rid of this plague. With every advance of the German army the local Nazis become more brazen and more demanding.

Some mornings we find Russian leaflets everywhere, distributed during the night. They urge the population not to cooperate with the Germans, they promise that one day the Soviets will be back. Gradski and his gang collect the leaflets and bring them to the Germans, explaining that the Jews printed them and distributed them during the night. The Germans are delighted with such loyal subjects and thank them for their help. They promise to settle accounts with the Jews. But on this particular occasion they do nothing about it. They know that similar leaflets have been found not only in Jasionowka but throughout the entire region, and to punish the Jews they don't need this farfetched reason—or any reason at all.

Four more days go by. On July 22nd the murderers are in our town again. This time the "operation" is carried out by the Polish Commandant Kovacki and his lieutenants—the miller Chmielewski, Gradski and Postmaster Francsewicz. They have a fine gift ready for the Gestapo—David Itzkowicz, the owner of a mill, who has become the victim for various reasons, including business competition, a rivalry dating back to the years before the war.

First they beat him up. Then they lock him up. Always a resourceful man, Itzkowicz manages to remove a stone from the wall of his cell and escape. It does not take long before the whole town knows what has happened. A man-hunt is organized. Itzkowicz has run to the cemetery and is hiding among the bushes and the gravestones. The hunters find a scent and go after their prey, but can't find him. Soon, however, the chase is over. When they bring him into town, his face is unrecognizable. A double guard is place over him.

As usual, one victim is not enough for the Gestapo. While they are at it they bring in Shimon Sherer, an artist who suffers from tuberculosis. The third victim is Zaydl Kulewski. They are all taken to Bialystok and shot. More and more we realize that the same fate awaits us all, yet everyone tries to find a good hiding place, make himself invisible.

Every few days the Germans arrive to "requisition" beds, pillows, blankets. And though the Jews have hardly anything left in their homes, they still must continue to be the suppliers. Kovnacki and Gradski soon learn from the Germans. Now the Jews must keep them satisfied too. Kovnacki demands that the Jews renovate his home. He also wants them to install a large baking oven. They do it for him willingly, hoping it will keep him quiet. If he becomes a bakery owner, maybe he will give up his position as town commandant and stop turning Jews over to the Germans.

Every day dozens of Jews report to him for work, even though they will not be paid for it. When the renovations are complete, he demands furniture, curtains, kitchenware. Frau Kovnacki needs only a few more pots and pans. And a cuspidor, which cannot be bought anywhere. Had our town not been looted and burned, all this might not have been much of a problem. But now these things are difficult to find. Here and there Jews find household goods they had buried to protect them against fire. When they finally supply everything that was ordered, Frau Kovnacki finds a flaw in the cuspidor—some of the enamel is chipped. And intelligent, capable Jews must occupy themselves with such nonsensical affairs because their lives and the fate of their families depend on it.

Several weeks more go by. It is becoming almost impossible to stand the strain any longer. The young people in general are nowhere to be seen. At that point Joseph Rosenblum begins to devote himself to our problem. About fifty years old, he is very shrewd and highly respected by both Jews and non-Jews in our town. He organizes a campaign to collect money and valuables for a community fund. Misha Lipshitz offers to help him. Together they collect a total of 5000 rubles and twenty American dollars. Kovnacki is still terrorizing the community. Perhaps his greed can be stilled by giving him a large sum of money. Rosenblum brings it to him in the name of Jasionowka's Jews, with a request that as commandant of the town he intervene with Germans not to inflict any further harm on its Jewish population.

Again it is quiet for a little while. In order to keep Kovnacki pacified they bring him new gifts every few days—shoe leather, foodstuffs, whatever they can find. Some of the young people reappear. But the community is carrying heavy burdens. Large sums of money have to be raised. The Germans, too, have to be bribed. A committee of two people is not sufficient to accomplish all this. A meeting is called. The committee is enlarged to seven.

It happened that at that time the Germans ordered the establishment of a Jewish "leadership body" that could act for the town's Jews—the so-called *Judenrat*, or Jewish Council. No one volunteers for that service, however, and thus the committee of seven has no choice but to become the *Judenrat* of Jasionowka.

At that time our town did not yet have its own kommissar; we were subject to the authority of the Knyszyn kommissariat. One day the Germans ordered all Jews to come out into the street for a roll-call. No one knows where they will be taken or when they will be brought back. The *Judenrat* tries to find out what the Germans want of us. Perhaps it is a trap. When the *Judenrat* learns that it is only a roll-call to select able-bodied men for work, they ask everyone to report. They themselves are first in line. Jews put on clean clothes and come out into the street.

Everyone wants to work. It is known that Jews who do not have jobs will be deported. Many of the town's factories had been burned down. There are not enough jobs for everyone in the town. Many of the younger men have gone off to find work in the villages as farm-hands, the older Jews as shepherds. Still, almost half remain unemployed. The *Judenrat* acts energetically on this and people begin to earn a little money. By various means they succeed in keeping everyone safe, for the time being.

In general, our situation has been made easier by the *Judenrat*. Now, when money has to be raised, it is done by them. All the *Judenrat* members work very hard. The president, Shlomo Schuster, manages things with a firm hand. Life in our town becomes a little more tolerable. Gradually people grow calmer, try to get to their jobs on time, carrying out orders no matter how difficult they are. But the demands of the Regional Kommissar are unreasonable. Not long after the roll-call he wants workers for the Kirchov road-building company, which has a very bad reputation in our area. It is not an ordinary labor camp; more like a death-camp. Rarely does anyone come back alive from there.

Again the town falls into a panic. It is clear that the authorities aim to kill off the rest of our young people, the few that are left. Again the *Judenrat* members travel to Knyszyn and explain that there is no one left in the town who is young and strong and who is not already working. But rational arguments are not enough here—other means are necessary. It takes a lot of money and extraordinary effort to do what needs to be done. But finally Jasionowka is exempted from the decree.

Soon another member is added to the Jewish Council—David Stolar. A clever, energetic man with a fluency in German, he has a special influence with the authorities. The non-Jews in Jasionowka, however, cannot bear this. Things have been too quiet for the Jews, for far too long.

So Bolek Bortnik, Alex Sokowicz and the estate owner Abramowicz make a special trip to Knyszyn. There they report to the Germans that they have discovered an important Communist activist in Jasionowka by the name of Velvl Trabanowski. A few days later Trabanowski is arrested and taken to Knyszyn. An ordinary working-man who had never been a Communist, he does not understand what they want of him.

At that point, the *Judenrat* receives its first blow. Joseph Rosenblum approaches the Polish workers and asks them to testify on behalf of Velvl Trabanowski. They refuse. They'd rather not do the Jews any favors. David Stolar takes this matter upon himself, disregarding the risk that he will get into serious trouble himself, since this is a political arrest.

But his efforts are in vain. People accused of that kind of crime never go free. Stolar decides to enlist the aid of the gendarme Heinkopof, who has a more lenient attitude toward Jews. The *Judenrat* gives him 10,000 marks and he promises to get Trabanowski released. It is wintertime. A snowstorm. Heinkopf takes Trabanowski into a woods, fires several shots into the air and tells Trabanowski to run and never come back to Jasionowka again. It should be recognized that Stolar deserves the credit for that.

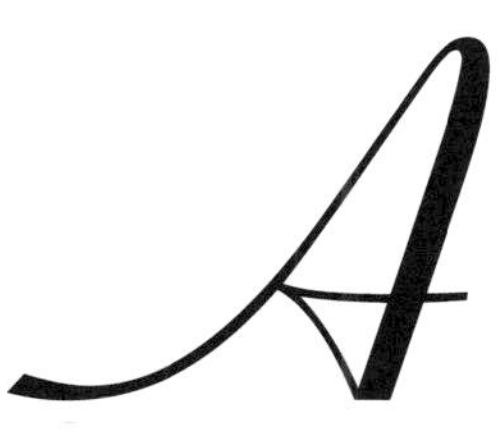

A few weeks go by "peacefully" with only a few "minor" interruptions, each of which takes several thousand marks out of our own depleted funds. The Jews keep sacrificing more and more necessities, however, so long as lives can be saved.

In the meantime, the news arrives that Jasionowka has been designated a "district" and will now have it own Kommissar. New problems. Under the old system we at least had a few hours respite from the Germans every day. But now—who knows what will happen. Maybe they will lock us into a ghetto too. But there is nothing we can do about it. With the previous kommissar we had established a bit of an agreement. We knew what he wanted, although that too, kept changing. One day he wanted a new fur coat for his wife. White woolen gloves. Brown rubber boots. And, it had to be nothing but the best. Who knows what the new Kommissar will want? At that time, it was a great comfort to know there was something with which we could bribe them.

Meantime, we are preparing a residence for the new District Kommissar. Renovations. Painting. All the work must be done by the Jews.

On June 22nd, the Kommissar arrives. His name is Vallu, a war invalid with a hunchback and sharp, bespectacled eyes. He begins to make known his demands and invites the *Judenrat* to his office. The first meeting is a good one. He receives them in a friendly manner. The members of the Council make a good impression on him. He promises to be favorable to the Jewish population. The only thing he wants in return is that we report punctually for work and carry out all his orders. He asks the *Judenrat* to call together all the Jews of Jasionowka and tell them that if anyone has a request of him, they should go through the Council and it would get to him.

What kind of work do the Jews do for the Germans? Everything is possible. Nothing is too difficult. All winter, shoveling the snow off the roads. Cutting down trees in the forest. Building, hauling, chopping firewood. Whatever is required of them, they do without complaining. Gradually, they become accustomed to it. Human dignity has disappeared a long time ago. All orders are carried out automatically. We stay alive only because they still allow us to do so.

The non-Jews in the town, however, do not like the idea of the new Kommissar being on such good terms with the Jews. They try to win his sympathy. They arrange a party for him in Kovnacki's home. But David Stolar has also been visiting the Kommissar, who likes to talk with him, and even invites him to Kovnacki's party. No matter what the Poles do to tear down Stolar's prestige, they fail. But they keep on trying and finally concoct something where even the Kommissar's friendship is not enough.

Since the *Judenrat* supplies everything the Kommissariat needs, and those needs cannot be met in Jasionowka, they must go to Bialystok. This is the task of Shlomo Schuster and David Stolar, who make the trip to Bialystok in a factory wagon which transports animal hides. The drivers, however, also transport illegal Polish nationalist literature. One of them, the peasant Kolinowski, is observed by a German office worker hiding a package of literature in the horse's feedbag. She reports it. And although Schuster and Stolar did not travel back to Jasionowka in that wagon, Kovnacki takes advantage of the situation to inform the Gestapo that the nationalist literature is printed in the Bialystok ghetto, and that Stolar brings it into Jasionowka. Meanwhile, the two *Judenrat* members have not even returned yet from Bialystok.

In the middle of the night, we hear shooting. The shots grow louder. We are certain that in the neighboring street the Germans have already shot all the Jews, because that's the way it happened in other places when they had some pretext. No one expects to live till morning. We can see people running into the fields in their nightclothes. We hear people crawling around in the darkness, searching for a hiding place. With the first signs of dawn, we discover that the Gestapo has arrived, along with some Russian ex-NKVD agents who are now serving the Germans. The Gestapo has been shooting indiscriminately to confuse and provoke the Jewish population.

They arrest David Stolar. Then they pick up the other members of the Jewish Council. They begin an intensive search for Shlomo Schuster, who left the house during the shooting. The chaos is indescribable. The young people have fled. No one reports for work that morning. No one even thinks about the consequences of that act of rebellion because everyone is certain that this provocation is an excuse to kill us all.

David Stolar's wife, a bright, intelligent woman, is desperate enough to go and ask the Gestapo why they have arrested her husband. They promise they will release him in exchange for 15,000 *zloty*. The entire Jewish population responds generously. Whoever has a penny hidden away brings it forward, because aside from the fact that his own life is not at stake, Stolar is regarded as a self-sacrificing "angel" who has gotten many Jews out of trouble. A considerable sum is raised.

Meanwhile, Stolar is released for a half-hour at a time, on condition that he return to custody. The Gestapo really expected him to flee, which would have provided the pretext for slaughtering all the Jews of Jasionowka. Knowing this, Stolar promises the Jews that he will not run away. "How can I? I am already in their hands. This is the last time I will see you." Still, everyone hopes that with the payment of the ransom, the Gestapo will let him go free again.

The required sum is collected and Masha Stolar brings it to the Gestapo. The same Germans, who only a few hours earlier had spoken to her so politely, now change their tune. They want one "trifling" thing from her in addition to the money—she must swear that the money is from the *Judenrat* treasury and that it had been assigned for Communist activities. And furthermore, that her husband is a member of the Communist Party. As soon as she signs the statement, David Stolar will be freed.

Masha, who knows that such a statement is tantamount to a death warrant for all the Jews of the town, absolutely refuses to do what they ask. However, one cannot simply "refuse" to do something the Gestapo asks—their methods of persuasion are very effective. One the verge of unconsciousness, she still refuses to sign such a paper. They continue their tortures until she finally loses her mind. Then they put a pen in her hand and forced her to sign her name.

(Those who saw her when she left the Kommissariat did not recognize her. Aside from her physical appearance, Masha Stolar, who had once walked so proudly and erectly, was now nothing more than an abject rag. Even her voice was unrecognizable. Still, she had enough presence of mind left to warn the Jews that she had just signed their death warrant and urged them all to try to escape.)

How terrible the consternation is! The Jews now know there is nowhere to run to. In the beginning there were still peasants in the villages who would let a Jew hide in a stable. (Some of them believed that things could change and the Russians might eventually return.) Now they are sure that the Germans will win the war. So, no one wants to open his door to a Jew. It is July, however, and one can hide for a while among the cornstalks.

A half-hour later there isn't a Jew left in Jasionowka. The Gestapo rides into town in their cars looking (they say) for one of their men who had vanished and then turned up wounded. Had there been any Jews in the town they would not have remained alive for long. The fear is so great, however, that even the next day, after the Gestapo has left, taking David Stolar with them, no one returns to their homes. The Kommissar tries to find at least one Jew, in order to calm the population. The police keep calling for anyone at all to appear, but no one does, until Michal Sapoznik finally turns himself into the Kommissar, who promises him that no one else will be hurt, that if the Jews want things to return to "normal" they must all report for work. Again, the Jews decide to come back. Those with jobs, report for work.

The *Judenrat* calls a meeting to discuss what to do to help Stolar. They decide to do everything possible, even at the risk of their own lives. After much traveling around and making inquiries, Shlomo Schuster learns that Stolar has been taken to Lik. Now the question becomes how to get him out of there, first to bring him back to Bialystok, where the matter would be easier to deal with. After three weeks of work, risking communication with certain people who represent danger to Jews, they succeed in having Stolar transferred to the prison in Bialystok.

But here a fresh series of troubles begins. After much effort, with money distributed on all sides, they are still unable to get him released.

In David Stolar we have lost a truly sympathetic leader, a man who risked his own life many times in order to help the community. All honor to his memory.

With Stolar no longer among us, our town is like a ship without a rudder. Schuster is totally occupied in trying to get him released. There is no one available to do anything for the community. The regional kommissar, like all other German officials, continues to make many demands on us, and they must all be fulfilled. He is dissatisfied with the house he has been living in and wants to build himself a palace. Many Jews are working on it—men, women and children. In addition, the kommissar has a weakness—every few days he must meet with all the Jews in Jasionowka. And once a week there is a roll call. And with each roll call there is a new fear for our lives.

Around this time a Zionist representative comes to our town and speaks with Shlomo Schuster, Yankl Dansky and Joseph Rosenblum. He brings news. The Germans have deported some of the Jews from the Warsaw Ghetto. For a long time it was not known where they were taken to. Now it has become all too clear. They were taken to a place called Treblinka, put to death in gas chambers and their bodies burned in a crematorium. He also reports that there is an organization now whose purpose is to help Jews arm themselves and not

The Germans have deported some of the Jews from the Warsaw Ghetto. For a long time it was not known where they were taken to. Now it has become all too clear. They were taken to a place called Treblinka, put to death in gas chambers and their bodies burned in a crematorium.

allow themselves to be taken without resistance. This organization has learned that some kind of resistance action has been planned for November in Bialystok.

New fears. Our fate is certain. The *Judenrat* tries to bolster the spirit of the community and gradually prepare the Jews to think about the reality now facing us. A member of the *Judenrat* goes to Bialystok to learn what is happening there. But the troubles of today do not allow us to think about tomorrow. The kommissar has demanded workers for a camp near the railroad station at Manke. Again we are ordered to line up in the street. The kommissar examines us and selects those he wants. All around us stand people from the villages who have heard that they can come into town and take Jews to work for them. So they too are looking us over with an eye for strong bodies. They are not doing this out of friendship for the Jews. They are simply using the opportunity to get a good farm hand free. It is like buying a slave. The only difference here is that the "buyer" does not even have to pay anybody for the "merchandise." How insignificant and degraded each Jew feels, even though he may be the wisest, most educated person in the world. They pick and choose us like horses in the marketplace. Yet it is much better to work for a farmer in the village than to go to some labor camp.

The Jewish Council decides to deal with this problem. With great effort and large sums of money (plus a caracul coat) they are successful in preventing the deportation. The kommissar keeps boasting how well he is treating his Jews and again promises that as long as he is in charge here nothing bad will happen to them. Yet he doesn't let an opportunity pass to torment us, to squeeze more and more out of us.

Up until now there have been no gendarmes in Jasionowka. This week four appear. Now a new period begins. We must "provide" for them too. One of them, Hugo Koch, demands that we supply him with "real" coffee. Should even one day pass that we don't bring him his coffee he bursts into Rosenblum's house and smashes things with his truncheon. Once, for the same "offense," he smashed Michal Sapoznik's fingernails. Jews must provide everything. The Polish police start leading the German gendarmes around the town on fresh searches. And there is no one to stop them.

Our economic situation is very bad. Jews are not permitted to go out into the villages or to speak with the farmers. They have no way to earn any money. They are not paid for the forced labor

How insignificant and degraded each Jew feels, even though he may be the wisest, most educated person in the world. They pick and choose us like horses in the marketplace. Yet it is much better to work for a farmer in the village than to go to some labor camp.

that they do for the Germans. They even have to take up collections to pay off the foremen so they will stop beating up the Jewish workers. One of those foremen, for the slightest "infraction,"—or for none at all—loves to administer seventy lashes. When the blood starts to flow and the victim falls unconscious, he prescribes a week's "vacation."

We are fair game for everybody. The peasant Grajewski, who serves as a spy for the Germans, reports to the kommissar that Zelik Halperin has bought a calf in the village and had it slaughtered. The kommissar arrests Halperin and decides that for such a crime he must be shot. And as a warning to all the other Jews, he orders them to be present at the execution. Not all the Jews appear, but some must attend, in order not to infuriate the kommissar still further. He stands the condemned prisoner up against the wall. Halperin's wife faints. His children cry. The kommissar pulls out his revolver—he will carry out this sentence himself. At the very last moment he accedes to the pleas of the *Judenrat* president. He fires a few shots into the air. Then he pistol-whips Halperin so badly that for several weeks he is confined to bed.

Autumn is in the air. Spirits are at their lowest. It is no help to us that the Germans are not advancing on the war fronts as rapidly as they did before. For the time being, they are still victorious.

Suddenly, a new decree. Not from the regional kommissar, but this time from higher up. Ghetto. All the Jews must be locked up in one place. This will hit us very hard. Most of the town has been burned down. We have already been living four to five families in one house. The kommissar makes a careful study of the town and announces that the ghetto will be located in a narrow street near the church. In no way can 250 families be squeezed into such a small area. Hygienic conditions will be out of the question.

The *Judenrat* attempts to convince the kommissar that there is no room in Jasionowka for a ghetto. He offers to send us to Knyszyn instead. Again, collecting money, gifts. Again, the kommissar promises to intercede for us with this superiors. A member of the *Judenrat* travels to Bialystok. Shlomo Schuster, who sees the situation clearly, pays more attention to the evacuation problem. From Yitzhok Engelman, the leader of the Jewish resistance, he learns that their "action" is planned for November.

All the Jews must be locked up in one place. This will hit us very hard. Most of the town has been burned down. We have already been living four to five families in one house.

The day scheduled for setting up our ghetto is approaching. Intervention is of no avail. The evacuation plan is proceeding at a rapid pace. Schuster returns to Jasionowka and calls the *Judenrat* together. They go to Knyszyn to consult with the Jewish Council there; perhaps they can do something. There are still some optimists around who refuse to believe that it will happen. Indeed, how could we have imagined such a thing? Cities and towns *Judenrein*?

In the evening we learn that wagons have already been procured to take the Jews to Knyszyn and Korycin. The last hope evaporates that we will survive this storm. Once more the *Judenrat* tells the kommissar what they have heard. He "guarantees" them that no harm will befall his Jews even if all the other Jewish towns are liquidated. We have no choice but to believe him, but the apprehension persists.

The next day, the second of November, everyone is out in the streets. A non-Jew comes from Knyszyn and tells us that he was allowed into that town, that it is surrounded by Gestapo. From inside Knyszyn he had heard the sound of shooting. Convinced that they will soon be coming for us, many Jews fled Jasionowka. Others walk around the streets waiting for the end. The *Judenrat* tries by telephone to find out from Bialystok what's going on. (There was a telephone in the main office of the leather factory.) The German clerk, not knowing that it is Jews who are on the telephone, informs them that the entire region is being cleared of Jews. They will all be evacuated. We cannot understand why they have not come for us yet. And where have the kommissar and his entire staff disappeared to? Not one German is visible.

At noon the kommissar rides up to the *Judenrat* office. He has good news, he announces. He has succeeded in saving his Jews. He is delighted with his achievement. As a working class town, Jasionowka will be exempted from the latest decree. All the other Jewish towns are being evacuated to labor camps near the Black Sea.

Feelings of relief and anxiety. No one trusts him. We are on a tiny island surrounded by a hostile sea; at any moment we can be washed away. It would not even require a heavy storm; a light breeze would be sufficient. How difficult it is to live through each hour, knowing that all around us there are no more Jews left. It is our own autumn. We are all dying, surrounded by a world of strangers.

We are on a tiny island
surrounded by a hostile sea;
at any moment
we can be washed away.
It would not even require
a heavy storm;
a light breeze would
be sufficient.
How difficult it is
to live through each hour,
knowing that
all around us there are
no more Jews left.
It is our own autumn.
We are all dying,
surrounded by a world
of strangers.

The next morning we learn that the Bialystok ghetto has not been touched, but the kommissar will no longer permit the Jewish Council members to go there. Jews from all over the villages are brought into Jasionowka. No Jew is allowed to leave the town. We are now a labor camp.

On the third day after the evacuation the first refugee comes to us, a Jewish woman from Wasilkow. Having been living in a village, she eluded the dragnet. Although the kommissar has forbidden Jews from other places to come to Jasionowka, she is of course welcomed by us. But the question still remains: how to make her presence legal. The *Judenrat* goes to the kommissar and somehow succeeds in registering her; he even permits us to accept other Jews. We realize that this is a trap to get together all the Jews in one place where it will be easy to find them.

During the next few days more Jews, who have been hiding in the woods and fields nearby, join us. We receive them hospitably. Every family takes in one or two people and they are added to the kommissar's list of workers in Jasionowka. All this means more "gifts" for him as we try to find out how much longer he will help us. Why are we really being allowed to stay here? He continues to reassure us that he is our protector. No doubt he senses that certain members of the Jewish Council no longer trust him. Although the *Judenrat* cannot go to Bialystok, they manage to send a messenger to the Council there. But Engineer Barash, the president, has learned nothing new from the German authorities with whom he is in touch. His advice to us is that if we think something is keeping us "safe" then we should just continue to do whatever we are doing.

Meanwhile our kommissar continues to pose as our savior and says he "can do more for us than Churchill." Knowing very well that the Jews don't trust him, he begins finding pretexts for searching the homes of various *Judenrat* members during the night, to see whether they are still sleeping there. Rumors also reach him that the *Judenrat* is advising anyone who can do so to leave Jasionowka. It is wintertime, however, and the Jews in the surrounding towns who have tried to hide in the villages have had to come back because the farmers there refused to give them shelter. We have already taken in a few dozen Jews from Trestyn who wandered around for seven-eight weeks among the peasants and then came to Jasionowka, filthy and crawling with lice. This further breaks our spirit and heightens the feeling of hopelessness. Our only ray of hope is that perhaps we can last until spring, when it will be easier to survive in the woods and fields. Who could have imagined then that one could stay alive in a ditch in the field for such a long time?

As the days go by, we continue to hear stories from the Poles that wagons are on the way to evacuate us from Jasionowka. One man knows for a fact that by the 15th we will all be gone. Another says with equal certitude that the date is the 20th. Whether these rumors are founded on fact or not, they give us no rest, they confuse and disturb us. People lose interest in life; the general feeling is that our days are numbered, no matter what. Are we more sinful than the other Jews that we have to suffer this living hell longer than anyone else?

By this time, there are some four hundred refugees in Jasionowka. The Polish police, seeing what happened in the other Jewish towns, and knowing that the same fate awaits us, go to all the Jewish families and take whatever they can squeeze out of them—money, furniture, clothing, bedding. Nobody stops them. Nobody even complains to the *Judenrat* any longer or expects them to intervene. We know we are all half-dead anyway and we don't want to fight for such trivial inconsequential things. People who will hear about what we experienced will no doubt wonder why we allowed it to happen. The Germans know the answer to that. If anyone resists, the entire Jewish community is held responsible and is punished, no matter how slight the infraction. And for the Germans, this was only a means of entertainment, a kind of sport. As for property and possessions, we will certainly take nothing of that with us, although the kommissar has assured us again and again that all those who have been evacuated are alive. Only their places of residence have been changed. By this time, we know different.

The kommissar's palace is now completed. Whenever commissions come to examine the work, the kommissar reports that the Jews did all the construction, that his Jews are very skilled craftsmen and that they are doing essential work for him. By Christmas-time his home is furnished with the finest furniture, curtains, and all the rest. He is still promising Mrs. Stolar that he will get her husband released soon. Not that she or anyone else believes him. We know it is more likely that the Germans will come and take us away, not that they will bring him back to us.

A bit of hope awakens in us when we hear the news from the front. We rejoice in the German defeat at Stalingrad. Their retreat is a source of great satisfaction for us. But at the same time, we are also afraid that it will only hasten our own destruction. Using whatever information is available to us, we try in every way possible to maintain our own existence, to win more time. We are certain that the German defeat is inevitable; what is not at all certain is that we will live to see it. Our will to stay alive until that moment becomes an obsession. Our salvation seems so close at hand. But will it come in time?

People who will hear about what we experienced will no doubt wonder why we allowed it to happen. The Germans know the answer to that. If anyone resists, the entire Jewish community is held responsible and is punished, no matter how slight the infraction. And for the Germans, this was only a means of entertainment, a kind of sport.

The peasants are saying that the Red Army is already at Minsk, that the Russians are already on Polish soil. Some of the villagers have begun to visit Jews again, to act in a more friendly manner. Some Jews are making arrangements for hiding places on farms in the area. Hope rises in our hearts, even though we know we are on a sinking ship that can go down to the bottom at any moment.

Nevertheless, we grow more optimistic. The young people are determined to resist if the Germans try to deport us. Better to be shot while resisting or running away. We even go out into the forest to try and dig trenches where we can hide. But our feet leave tracks in the snow. And the ground is too frozen to dig. If only spring would come, then we would all escape to the woods. We begin to discuss seriously the question of obtaining weapons, a very difficult task.

Then suddenly, on January 21, several cars full of Germans drive into the marketplace. They seem to be studying the topography of the town. People start running. But we are in the dead of winter; there is nowhere to hide for even twenty-four hours. The kommissar and the gendarmes ride through every street, ordering people back into their homes. Again the kommissar assures us we are safe here, we have nothing to fear. But no one really believes him—until the cars leave Jasionowka.

The next morning, those Jews who had fled return with the demoralizing news that they could find absolutely nowhere to hide. There is no escape. It is nightmarish to live with this knowledge. They also bring news that this time the victims of the Gestapo were a Gypsy family in the village of Bobrowka.

Saturday, January 22. Yesterday we learned that the ghetto in Grodno has been liquidated. We now realize that the Gestapo had probably come for us, but noticing that Jews were running away, they had postponed the "action" for another time. Will this be our last Sabbath in Jasionowka? The mood is one of utter hopelessness. No one smiles. The only thing people can talk about is whether they will still be among the living next Sabbath. Yet no one runs away, because they will perish in any case. And there is always the possibility that the kommissar will still be able to keep his promise.

Sunday. We keep trying to find out from the kommissar what his plans are for us. In the evening a Gestapo car appears. We know that the deportations usually take place on Mondays. Again, several *Judenrat* members go to see the kommissar. They wait until the late hours of the night and learn nothing new except that the Gestapo has left.

But at four in the morning, three hundred Gestapo troops ride into Jasionowka in trucks and station themselves all over the town. Now it is too late to run. They take the Jewish Council members into custody. The Polish police are working right alongside the Gestapo, driving the Jews out into the streets. Gradski is in his glory.

It is a bitterly cold morning. People are running to and fro in panic. Only a few have prepared hiding places. We are already more dead than alive. Fathers are attending their own funerals with their children and grandchildren. How terribly barbaric it is—a whole town, a whole people is dying, condemned to death as if they were the most depraved criminals. There is no difference between rich and poor, old or young. Mothers with infants in their arms, half-frozen. Children beg for a bit of warmth. Mothers' hearts break.

Fathers are attending their own funerals with their children and grandchildren. How terribly barbaric it is—a whole town, a whole people is dying, condemned to death as if they were the most depraved criminals. There is no difference between rich and poor, old or young.

The Jewish homes are empty except for the Gestapo and Polish police who are searching wildly in all the corners. When they find old or sick people confined to bed they shoot them on the spot. When they find someone hiding they drive them out into the street and shoot them before the eyes of everyone. Albin Shach, a villager, leads the Gestapo to the home of Hillel Radzi, our Mayor. (Shach himself had been living there!) No one feels sorry now for those who have perished; if anything, we envy them, because their suffering is over. Some Jews try to run away and are shot. The Gestapo doesn't waste a moment. At mid-day Jews are still standing in the streets, numb with cold. Hungry children are crying. The Gestapo runs around using their truncheons and their rifle butts. Gradually, like vultures around a corpse, some of the villagers and townspeople begin looting Jewish homes of whatever is left. This is their last opportunity. They are now getting even with the kommissar too.

One Jew, hiding in a Polish home, overhears this conversation. A woman is describing how dreadful it was when the Jews were being driven out into the street. Another woman consoles her: "Don't worry. We'll get used to it. It will be much better without them." And she gazes fondly at her Jewish neighbor's home, which she has long pictured as her own. Every Pole in town has already selected a Jewish home for himself. They consider themselves the rightful owners. Their day has come. There are a few, however, who believe that when the Germans have finished with the Jews they will start the same game with the Poles. But mostly the non-Jews are pleased with the things have turned out. There is one problem, though: many Jews are still not out there in the street. So they go out to help search for them.

In the meantime, the Jews in the street provide free entertainment. Everyone runs out to watch. The transport vehicles are beginning to arrive.

The last act. The play is ending. Insane scenes. Shouts. Commands. Spasmodic screams. The wailing is indescribable. It is difficult to part with life when one is young and strong. And only because there is a megalomaniac named Hitler in the world with sadistic needs and with the drive to rule over all Europe. Greater Deutschland! *Judenrein!* As a gift to his people—the elimination of the Jews. Yes, he is winning on our front, but this is not how it will end.

All the condemned stand in the street thinking about only one thing: perhaps before the end of the day we shall no longer exist. Tomorrow at the latest. Gone are the days of miracles. There is no possibility of help. Now we long for only one thing: to know what the end of this terrible story will be. If only a few of us could survive somewhere as avengers. To see to it that Jews in the rest of the world never forget. Let no one desecrate the holiness of revenge. Jews are a people of mercy, quick to forgive. But about this, they must not be silent. The world must be filled with a storm of outrage. Everyone with a human heart and mind must help in the sacred task. Otherwise, no one will ever be able to imagine what happened, the bestial things the Germans did.

The Gestapo is still searching all over the town for hidden Jews. Their helpers are equally assiduous. Jerumin Sadowski runs around like a mad dog, yelling that he knows where all the Jews are hiding. Jews who still have family in hiding-places shiver in terror. Bolek Franczkel marches around with his rifle, also hunting for Jews in hiding. And he gets angry when he can't find any (even though they can see him through a crack in the wall). Walenchuk runs into Joseph

Rosenblum's house and drags out his mother, a woman of eighty. When she picks up a blanket to cover herself, he tears it out of her hands and drives her out into the cold, swearing filthy oaths at her for her audacity.

In many instances non-Jews dragged people out of barns and stables and beat them half to death. And in order to please kommissar, they then dragged them out into the middle of the street. No one offers a child a crust of bread, or even a kind word. With hateful laughter, they accompany the Jews from their homes. Sarah Kaminsky, an older woman, falls dead in the street. They toss her body into a pile of snow.

If all this had happened suddenly, unexpectedly, people would have run around half-demented. Now they are only bewildered. Children look at their parents for help, but all the grownups are just as helpless. Mothers uncover their shivering infants—let them not suffer so much. Why was it taking so long, anyway?

But this is no accident, all this waiting out in the cold. It is being executed according to the Nazi system.

No one feels sorry now for those who have perished; if anything, we envy them, because their suffering is over.

Now they have crowded us all onto sleighs. We are leaving our town, our homes, our favorite streets, our dreams. We want to kiss the earth, to cry, to scream, to resist. Why is this happening? Are we such evil people? And what of the children? The children!

Some people have become silent, motionless, almost not breathing. Only their eyes speak. They turn their heads for a last look at the town, their home from which they are being driven at the point of a gun.

A long line of sleighs. Alongside the sleighs walk the armed Gestapo guards. Any disobedience of their rules will be punished. Everyone knows what that means.

We travel a distance of one kilometer and there is a command to halt. We have been out in the frost since dawn. No one is permitted to get off the sleigh, to take a few steps, to warm oneself up in the bitter cold. For a half hour the sleighs just sit there. Then we start again. Then we stop for another half hour. In this way, the trip to the railroad stations, which usually takes an hour by sleigh, lasts nine hours. The stopping and starting—there is no reason for that except to torture

If only a few of us could survive somewhere as avengers. To see to it that Jews in the rest of the world never forget. Let no one desecrate the holiness of revenge. Jews are a people of mercy, quick to forgive. But about this, they must not be silent. The world must be filled with a storm of outrage.

us still further. Nine hours in an open sleigh in this weather—our hands and feet are frostbitten. We could not walk or run even if we tried.

The trains are ready for us—freight cars with closed doors. They herd us into the cars like cattle—one hundred and fifty people in a car—and the guards bolt the doors from the outside.

The air is suffocating. The darkness is total. People step on one another. Sounds of muffled weeping—people have no strength left even to cry. It becomes difficult to breathe. The train stops. The door is opened. Someone throws a few loaves of bread into the car. They demand payment of a hundred marks for each loaf. Mothers, fathers, struggle over the bread—not for themselves, but for the children, to ease their hunger pains a little.

The door is locked again. The train starts moving. People begin reciting their last confession. Some devout Jews murmur in broken tones that if anyone survives this they will no longer believe in God anyway, for permitting such a thing to happen to us. One man faints. People try to revive him; others stop them—why not let him die in peace? Several of the older people die on the trip. Someone tries to open a window near the ceiling to let some air in.

Mordecai Schuster gets an idea. He urges the younger people to escape through the window. The train is racing at full speed, but what do they have to lose? Either way, they will die. But how to get up to the window and crawl out? Schuster, with those strong young people around him, cannot keep still. He helps them climb up. Not only the young people should try, he insists, but anyone who can still move his legs. He keeps repeating: "Remember! Avenge us!"

Soon only the older people and the young children are left in the car. In other cars they are doing the same thing.

A young father bids farewell to his wife and child and lights a match to look at them for the last time. He takes the child's hat as a keepsake. How harrowing it is to watch such scenes!

None of those who remained inside the trains ever returned. How agonizing their deaths were we do not know. But those who "escaped" also faced an uncertain end. Many were injured jumping off the moving trains. Then they had to look for partisans in the forest. But first they had to find a little warmth so they wouldn't freeze to death.

A young father bids farewell to his wife and child and lights a match to look at them for the last time. He takes the child's hat as a keepsake. How harrowing it is to watch such scenes! None of those who remained inside the trains ever returned. How agonizing their deaths were we do not know. But those who "escaped" also faced an uncertain end.

One small group met in the forest. A young man recalls a farmer named Wisocki who lives close by, in a village near Merezkes. He knows Wisocki and believes he can be trusted. They decide to risk it. They find his house and he receives them hospitably enough, but is afraid to let them stay in his house because the Germans have warned the population that the penalty for providing shelter to a Jew is death. He is willing to let them stay in the cellar, however.

While they are in the cellar he rides to Knyszyn and returns with German gendarmes. They take the Jews to the prison in Bialystok and shoot them.

Others who leaped from the train find shelter with farmers who let them stay a few days, squeeze all the money they have out of them, and then order them to leave. Nine people find shelter in the village of Kamianka with the farmer Kolaska. He treats them well, then goes to Jasionowka and brings the police. All nine are shot. By some miracle, Beylke Goldfarb is only wounded. Holding her breath, she is taken for dead—and stays alive. The gendarmes leave and tell the villagers to take the bodies to the Jewish cemetery in Jasionowka. The peasants strip the dead of their clothing—even their underwear—then put them in a wagon and take them to the cemetery. Beylke waits until they leave, then walks back to the village. No one lets her in. Somehow she makes her way to the Bialystok ghetto.

In the meantime, people have been searching in vacant Jewish homes for hidden wealth. In David Radzin's house they discover a bunker where twenty Jews have been hiding. Sabin Kurczewsky is about to run to the Germans to report it. The Jews offer him a gold watch, but it doesn't stop him. He runs to the kommissariat. Meantime the Jews find another hiding place. When the police arrive they search all over but cannot find them. They do, however, find David Woyczowsky, who has been living for six days on raw peas, but was discovered by Olga Leschinski and reported to the kommissar.

In the same way, Mitiek Klaga of Czarniczak turns over Benjamin Kulik, a 15-year old Jewish boy, to the Polish policeman Gawkowksi, who shoots the boy without even taking him to the kommissariat.

The peasant Baristowski catches Abraham Moshe Azeh, ties him up and brings him in a wagon to the kommissariat, where he is shot.

Shmuel Shapiro, badly beaten by the peasant Kolosa in the village of Bobrowka, runs in a dazed state to the village of Jaswily in the middle of the day. The villagers take him to Jasionowka, where he is shot.

The peasant Sokol from Rameyke reports to the Germans about a bunker which Jews constructed in a woods. The Germans surround the area and blow up the bunker with grenades, killing Leib and Rivka Marenberg, Itzik Weisberg, Abraham Yitzhok Glagowski and a man from Warsaw, name unknown.

Kazulska of Woytowuc brings Noteh Rabinowicz to Jasionowka, where he is shot.

Mietek Klaga brings another sacrifice to the Germans—the brothers Tanchum and Lazer Sapoznik, who had come to the village of Czarniczak to buy bread.

In the village of Krukoszczyzna the two Lengewicz brothers capture the Gapesenski brothers, refugees from Suchawala, bring gendarmes from Korycin to shoot them.

The peasants Kalinowski and Wilczka attack Alter Manowski and his wife and daughter. They chop off the heads of the couple with axes, but the daughter manages to escape.

The peasant Magderczuk betrays a bunker in the Kopiska forest where the Bratstein family has been hiding. Bratstein and his two children are shot. His wife escapes and at night runs to the home of Stczepanski, a farmer whom she knows very well. Instead of helping her, he takes her forcibly to the kommissariat, where she is shot.

Nisl Gerzowicz, Choneh Mikanski and Hershl Balberg come into the village of Krasne to buy bread. Felix Dubaniewicz and Loyniek Patafe bring Germans and police dogs. They tie the Jews to trees and let the dogs do the rest.

In general it is more difficult to hide from the village population than from the Germans. The Jews realize that it is impossible to hide in the villages. But spring is approaching. The weather is turning warmer and the ground in the forest is easier to dig. Camouflaged bunkers are prepared. Food is bought from villagers who are friendly to Jews. Still, the situation keeps growing more and more dangerous. Farmers coming into the forest for wood come upon traces of Jews and report it to the German authorities. Soldiers encircle the area and begin hunting down Jews as if they were wild animals.

Others who leaped from the train find shelter with farmers who let them stay a few days, squeeze all the money they have out of them, and then order them to leave.

The first to fall is Bibak Schuster and her five year old son Moyshele, who had been living in the woods so long that he knew the paths better than the grownups. Also killed at that time are Chaim Intrelgazur, a refugee from Zabludowka, Mula Simner from Knyszyn, Abraham Yitzhok Glazer and Zeydke Glazer.

The rest of the Jews now live in constant terror, moving from place to place, even though digging a trench under such circumstances is more difficult than building a whole house in normal times. Sometimes Jews start digging and have to stop in the middle to find a "safer" place. But they really have no choice.

Very soon there is another raid. Killed in that one are Zalman Krasnonski, Choneh Mikuczenek, Shmuel Kawike, Zeydka Padlipski and Hershl Balberg.

It becomes clear that to stay in the forest for any length of time without weapons is impossible. The Jews begin looking for a way to buy guns. They make contact with a farmer from the village of Karsne who helps them get what they need. This makes it easier to obtain food from those who are reluctant to sell it. They also feel a little safer from the Germans. This particular farmer turns out to be of invaluable help for the Jews living in the forest. He knows when the Germans are coming to hunt Jews and reports it to the Jewish leaders. Thanks to him a number of Jews escaped death at that time simply by leaving the area for a little while.

One group of Jews goes into the village of Bogne and are met by German gendarmes who had been informed about this and were waiting for them. A fight with the Germans ensues in which the Polish policemen Czizlewski and Slezinski are killed. But it also costs the lives of two young Jews, Chaim Tikacki and Moshe Borischewski.

Some of the Jews then move their hiding place to the village of Agrodnike, in a barn that belongs to a farmer named Niedzalkes. But it is not long before someone notices them and betrays them to the Germans, who come to the farm, surround the barn and burn it down with the Jews still inside it.

This horror completely shatters the spirit of those Jews who have survived, even though they keep hearing about Germany's military defeats. A few days later they learn that in the woods around them there are many partisans who are still in communication with the Red Army. The partisans do their work behind the lines. They tell us of a train, carrying important German leaders, which they derailed and damaged. This was the kind of news that revived our spirits again.

In the village of Baika the partisans execute the German gendarme, Hugh Koch, who couldn't get enough coffee from the *Judenrat* in Knyszyn and Jasionowka and who used to beat people for not wishing him a good morning. The next day he might beat someone else for saying good morning to him—how dare they! What satisfaction the Jews felt that they had lived to see him punished!

But even with liberation as close as it was, Jews still continued to be victimized. In the village of Dudke, Moshe Mahler and Munya Sidranski are badly beaten by a farmer named Dudke. One of them dies under the blows; the other is killed by the Germans the following morning.

Of the three hundred Jews who escaped from the trains, one hundred hid in bunkers. Of these, fifty-eight survived. (In comparison with other towns, this was a tremendous number.) Eventually they were rescued by the Red Army. Some saved themselves in the forest. Some lived with Polish farmers, who really risked their own lives. These were the rare exceptions among the Polish people. We owe them our gratitude. They are people who had a mission and carried it out to the end—with great difficulty and much suffering—and they too are martyrs of that time. To our sorrow, such people were very rare.

We must not and we will not forget them....

Post Script

And now, living in Mexico, thirty years after that monstrous inferno in Europe, it is finally possible to mention the names of those wonderful individuals who, with their sense of justice and humanity, made it possible for us to survive. We shall never, never forget them.

Vladek and Adolcia Boruta, who, under extremely difficult conditions, in the very center of the village of Kamianka, hid us for a year-and-a-half at the risk of their own lives.

There were four of us: Chaneh Rosenblum, Baile Schuster-Klatnitska and her daughter Roske, and myself, Feitche Schuster. Hoping every day, which dragged like an eternity, that it would soon come to an end, and hearing every day that the Germans were shooting Jews in other villages and in the forest (some Poles were exposing the location of the hiding places to the authorities), you can easily imagine how we felt.

For a period of time, the Borutas also gave shelter to Alter Freedman and his young son, who later fell in Israel in the War of Liberation.

The Dekar family in the village of Stoka, who themselves were very poor, gave shelter to four Jewish boys in a little stable. The boys survived under horrible conditions, but thanks to the Dekar family, they did manage to survive. These were: Reuven and Chone Gonionzki, Berl Schuster and Shimon Zlatarinski.

We are forever grateful also to the brothers Adolf and Juzek Kolosa, who owned a farm near Kamianka. Adolf, who at that time was the village magistrate and had contact with the Germans, nevertheless took the risk. Thanks to him, Maishe Schuster survived. (He had worked for them as a farm hand when that was still possible and permissible.) After the Jews were deported from Jasionowka, the Kolosa brother hid him, along with Benjamin Dembinski.

The farmer Wladislaw Czarnecki, from Meczarloki near Stoka, built a bunker in one of his stables and hid seven Jews in fairly decent living conditions. Among them were two who could not pay him any money at all. Those who survived here until the liberation were: Shlomo, Eliyohu-Chaim and Moishe Schuster, Yankl Dunski, Benjamin Halpern, Maishe Rosenblatt and Shmuel Waslikowski.

Czarnecki was the father of young children. The four older ones knew what was going on and understood the necessity of secrecy. They helped their parents in this difficult and dangerous task. The Czarneckis paid a heavy price for their courage. As soon as the war in that region was over and the Polish nationalists and anti-Semites began their agitation, they attacked the Czarnecki family in their home, killed Wladislaw's sister and burned down part of their farm. To get them away from this dangerous situation, the Schuster brothers moved them into the former German area of Stettin, where they settled down, rebuilt their homes and educated their children.

In our neighborhood, there were a few other Poles like these who kept alive a small group of Jews, and we shall never forget them for their courage and their kindness. Unfortunately, such individuals were the very rare exception.

F.S.
Mexico, 1978

NOTES ON THE DEATH OF MY SISTER, FEITCHE SCHUSTER

That Feitche would probably die by June or July of 1978, we knew ever since October 1977, when her cancer was discovered in Houston, Texas.

I went to Houston in October to meet with the doctors, and went there three more times between October 1977 and May of 1978. Our stays in Houston together were very meaningful since we were in adjoining rooms in a hotel and spent all the waking hours together. It gave us a chance to talk.

Feitche would insist on talking about what will be after she is dead. She worried about Schleime very much and did not know what he would do. She did not want him to be lonesome; she worried about his health. Her family—all of us—was her world and as she was preparing for her own death she would worry about our health and our happiness. No matter how sick she felt, she was always prepared to talk about my children and the Schwartz and Schuster children in Australia. Sad and difficult as our visits together were, they also provided great and meaningful experiences.

I also made three trips to Mexico—in February, April, and finally in June of 1978. In February, my wife Jane, and the kids—Debbie, Jamie, and Miriam went to Guadalajara with me and from Guadalajara we all—including Feitche and her husband Schleime, and my brother Maishe and his wife Madeleine—went to Puerto Vallarta for a vacation.

This was really the last time we enjoyed Feitche's company. She was still able to go down to the beach with us. She also went to town with us twice and had dinner in restaurants. She loved to sit on the beach and watch the children swim and play and have a good time. She loved to talk to the family, especially about the family during the war and pre-war years in the shtetl.

Feitche prepared for death as some prepare for a journey. For months she was occupied—sorting out old letters, rereading them, destroying those she did not care to save and turning over to me letters from family members she felt I should have. During the war she wrote an article about the liquidation of Jasionowka, our shtetl, and how she was compelled to add a postscript naming the Polish families who helped us out.

The last visit to Guadalajara, on June 22, 1978, was the most difficult one. From conversations with her doctors in Houston, I knew that she would probably die before the end of June. I was determined to be there when it happened, knowing that it might be the most painful experience of my life. Jane offered to go with me and we ended up going there together.

When we arrived at her house on Thursday, Feitche as much as said, "Did you come to see me die?" She knew the end was near. Nevertheless she was happy to see us.

The same Thursday afternoon, her doctor came over to the house to see Feitche and talk to us. He suggested that Feitche be taken to a hospital where the accumulation of fluids in her body could be removed in order to relieve pain. On Friday, he came again and the decision was made to take Feitche to the hospital the next morning.

As we were preparing to take Feitche to the car and transport her the few blocks to the hospital, she said that she would like to see all of the rooms in the house once more. She knew that this would be the last chance. Unfortunately, she was too weak even for that.

The procedure to remove the fluid was done and instead of relieving the pain, it made her pain and suffering even more unbearable. Between Saturday and the following Thursday, when she died, Feitche suffered terrible. The pain was more than she could stand, and she cried in agony. Schleime, her devoted husband, was in as much pain as she was. Tuesday, when Schleime broke down and cried, Feitche looked at him and said, "What are you crying like that for? I am not dying yet." He replied, "I am not crying because you are dying, but because you suffer so." I, too, found it more difficult to see her suffer as she did than from the realization that she was dying.

Over the years, most of the family in Guadalajara have not been close. Schleime's sister Zlatke and her husband, Avremel, have been over regularly. But now that Feitche was dying, the family drew closer. At the hospital, it seemed there were relatives waiting in the lobby all the time. Many friends also came, especially the Lonchiners (Manuel and Martha) who have been good friends for many years.

On Wednesday, June 28, it looked like Feitche would die that day. The doctor who came over to see her about 5:00 P. M., said that she was in the process of dying, and probably would be dead within two hours. He was surprised to find that she was still alive the next morning. Alive she was, but what a life! The pain was more than she could stand. She had periods when she seemed unconscious, followed by periods when she was perfectly lucid. Tuesday and Wednesday nights, Jane and I stayed in the hospital room with Feitche. Late Wednesday night when Feitche woke up and saw all of us in the room, she asked, "Why are you all here? I am not dying yet."

Even during these last few days, when Feitche would have a moment of less pain and be up, she was happy to hear about the children. When I told her about a letter from Australia, she wanted to know how the children were. When I told her that we called home, she again wanted to know how the children were and what they were doing. The family, and especially the children were her life and she showed her devotion to them until the last moment.

The last moment came on June 29, 1978, a Thursday, at 10:35 P. M. When she woke up Thursday she said to me, "Berele, today I am going to die." All day long she suffered, unable to breathe, asking for more oxygen, and screaming with pain. Later that evening, with her friends and family present, Feitche stopped breathing. Her face relaxed and, a moment later, so did her pulse. Thus, while I held her hand, my dear sister, whom I loved more than words can tell, departed from this earth, and took with her half of my being.

Bernard (Berl) Schuster, Rochester, NY
July 20, 1978

Berl's three siblings: Feitche, Maishe and Baile.
(1965)

Feitche, Rosie, Shleime and Baile
at a family wedding in Australia.
(1974)

Feitche, Deborah and Berl,
Jamie and Shleime in Rochester.
(1966)

Feitche with Berl's daughter,
Miriam, in Mexico.
(1972)

Feitche's gravesite in Jerusalem, Israel. Her husband, Schleime, emigrated there after her death in 1978.